Luftwaffe Fighters of World War Two

CHRIS GOSS

Front cover top image: Junkers Ju 88 R-2s of I Gruppe/Zerstörergeschwader 1, France, 1944.

Front cover bottom image: Messerschmitt Bf 109 E-3 of 1 Staffel/Jagdgeschwader 53 (JG 53), Rennes, August 1940. Unteroffizier Werner Karl (POW 2 Sep 40), Unteroffizier Willi Ghesla (POW 5 Oct 40) and Feldwebel Heinrich Höhnisch (POW 9 Sep 40).

Back cover inset image: Fw 190 A-0, Werk Nummer (Wk Nr) 0020 at Bremen, 1941.

Back cover main image: Messerschmitt Bf 109F-2s of 9 Staffel/JG 2, France, spring 1941.

Title page image: Oberleutnant (Oblt)Josef Wurmheller of 9./JG 2 standing alongside his Fw 190 A-6 Wk Nr 530314 coded yellow 2+I. With 78 victories on the rudder, this photograph was taken between 16 and 22 August 1943. This aircraft was destroyed in an air attack on Vannes, 23 September 1943.

Contents page image: Focke Wulf Fw 190 A-4s of Ergänzungs/Schnellkampfgeschwader 10 (SKG 10), Cognac, 1943.

Published by Key Books
An imprint of Key Publishing Ltd
PO Box 100
Stamford
Lincs PE9 1XQ

www.keypublishing.com

The right of Chris Goss to be identified as the author of this book has been asserted in accordance with the Copyright, Designs and Patents Act 1988 Sections 77 and 78.

Copyright © Chris Goss, 2023

Profiles on pp 8, 15, 57 and 68 are by Pete West

Profiles on pp 80, 85, 101, 105 and 111 © Andy Hays (www.flyingart.co.uk)

All colourisation provided by ColoursbyRJM

ISBN 978 1 80282 485 8

All rights reserved. Reproduction in whole or in part in any form whatsoever or by any means is strictly prohibited without the prior permission of the Publisher.

Typeset by SJmagic DESIGN SERVICES, India.

Contents

Introduction 4
Chapter 1   The First and the Last 5
Chapter 2   Sitzkrieg 22
Chapter 3   Zerstörer's 11-Month War 29
Chapter 4   Butcher Bird 36
Chapter 5   Fighter-Bombers Over Dieppe 43
Chapter 6   Stopgap Night-Fighters 48
Chapter 7   Junkers Fighters 55
Chapter 8   Zerstörers Over the Med 61
Chapter 9   Life and Death of an Ace 65
Chapter 10   One Man's *Barbarossa*: The Invasion of The Soviet Union as Experienced by a German Fighter Pilot 72
Chapter 11   Messerschmitt Me 210/410 Hornisse 78
Chapter 12   Dornier's Twin-Engined Arrow 85
Chapter 13   The Weird and the Wonderful 88
Chapter 14   Messerschmitt's Swallow 94
Chapter 15   Pocket Rocket 100
Chapter 16   Heinkel's Nocturnal Hunter 104
Chapter 17   Sparrow Goes to War 109
Chapter 18   Red Hearts Over Malta 115
Chapter 19   Night-Fighter Ace 122

Introduction

Eighty-three years after the outbreak of World War Two, the Luftwaffe still fascinates and interests many. The latest generation is keener than ever before to know more about something that affected and influenced their grandparents or great-grandparents, from both the Allied and German sides. Such names as Messerschmitt, Junkers, Heinkel, Dornier and Focke-Wulf are associated with German aircraft production and, in particular, fighters. Other names, such as Horten, Bachem and Blohm und Voss, are less well known. However, all designed, developed and built fighter aircraft, some of which fought right through the war; some fought for a matter of months at the end of the war and some arrived too late to go into combat. This book will give the reader a better insight into the Luftwaffe fighters of World War Two.

Bf 110D of III./Zerstörergeschwader (II.ZG 26) being worked on in North Africa, 1942.

Chapter 1
The First and the Last

At the start of World War Two, the Luftwaffe had two modern fighter aircraft available, namely the single-engined Messerschmitt Bf 109 and the twin-engined Bf 110. Both were still in action at the end of the war, albeit by then they were more powerful, had heavier armament and were being used in different ways than just as a day fighter.

Messerschmitt Bf 109

Designed by Professor Willi Messerschmitt and Robert Lusser for the Bayerische Flugzeugwerke AG (which would later become the Messerschmitt AG), the Bf 109 single-seat fighter was manufactured in larger numbers than any other warplane of World War Two. For much of the first two years of the war, the Bf 109E was generally considered superior to its opponents, albeit with the German fighter suffering some drawbacks that limited its full potential.

The requirement for a single-seat fighter was set by the German Ministry of Aviation, the Reichsluftministerium (RLM), in late 1933 and issued to German aircraft manufacturers in 1934. Messerschmitt's Rolls-Royce-Kestrel-powered Bf 109V1 first flew in September 1935 and the following month found itself being assessed against its rivals – the Heinkel He 112, Arado Ar 80 and Focke-Wulf Fw 159. Nevertheless, in March 1936, the RLM decided the Bf 109 would be its fighter of choice and full production began shortly afterwards.

By now, the Rolls-Royce engine had been replaced by a Junkers Jumo 210 engine, and after various prototypes, the initial production version, the Bf 109B-1 (known as the 'Berta'), began replacing the older fighters, such as the He 51 and Ar 64 in spring 1937. The B-1 variant was powered by a Jumo 210Da engine (the B-2 with the Jumo 210Ea) and was armed with two MG 17 machine guns on top of the engine and an engine-mounted MG 17 or MG FF cannon. Later B-2s were powered by the Jumo 210G engine. The Bf 109B would be sent to Spain to be part of the Condor Legion and was soon tested in combat.

Messerschmitt continued to develop its new fighter at pace. The Bf 109V8 was still powered by the Jumo 210Da but now had two guns fitted to the wings. The V8 was then the catalyst for the Bf 109D (the 'Dora'), which was powered with the Daimler-Benz DB 600Aa and which then resulted in the Bf 109E-1 (the 'Emil'), which began to appear at the end of 1938. The E-1 was powered by the DB 601A engine and armed with four MG 17 machine guns. Arriving on fighter units from spring 1939 onwards, it was the

Bf 109D, 1938.

Bf 109E-1, ably supported by a few Bf 109Ds, that formed both the backbone and teeth of the Luftwaffe's fighter force when war was declared.

Messerschmitt then fitted a DB 601Aa engine and replaced the wing machine guns with MG FF cannon, resulting in the Bf 109E-3. This was followed by the fitment of the MG FF Motorkanone (MG FF/M), which fired improved ammunition, resulting in the Bf 109E-4 (which also had improved armour plating and a more angular cockpit). The equipping of bombs to the Bf 109E began in July 1940, and by the end of the Battle of Britain, one Staffel per Gruppe was Jagdbomber – usually called 'Jabo' (literally fighter-bomber) – capable. Such aircraft had the suffix E-1/B, E-3/B or E-3/B and were fitted with an ETC 500 bomb rack. Towards the end of the Battle of Britain, a number of Bf 109E-4s were fitted with DB 601N engines and designated E-4/N. Also, a few Bf 109E-7s (which were the same as the E-4/Ns but able to be fitted with a 300-litre centre-line drop tank) and Bf 109E-8s (which were the same as the E-4s but fitted with a DB 601E engine) made an appearance before the end of 1940.

In October 1940, the Bf 109F (the 'Friedrich') made an appearance in the skies over England. Issued to Stab/Jagdgeschwader 51 (JG 51) and I./JG 51, it was the Geschwader Kommodore, Maj Werner Mölders, who claimed his 49th, 50th and 51st kills flying

Left: Bf 109B seen with a training unit, 1940.

Below: Bf 109B coded T+KB was written off in a training accident, 5 April 1943.

Bf 109Ds seen at Pardubitz, winter 1938.

a Bf 109F-1 over south-east England on the afternoon of 22 October 1940. Fitted with a DB 601N, the Bf 109F-1 looked different to the Bf 109E in that it had a cantilever tailplane, rounded wing tips, a redesigned and symmetrical cowling, retractable tail wheel and was armed with an engine-mounted MG FF/M and two MG 17s on the top of the cowling; the F-2 differed in the calibre of the guns.

The Bf 109E's Achilles' heel in the Battle of Britain was its limited operating range of just under 400 miles. To fly over the west of England, Bf 109E units had to position their forward base either at Cherbourg in northern France or in the Channel Islands. Then, as the phase of battle changed to attacks on London, almost all Jagdgeschwader moved to Pas-de-Calais but even then, London and the Thames Estuary was at the limit of the Emil's range, especially when time for combat (normally 15–20 minutes maximum and most flights were an hour's duration) was factored in. Most Bf 109s tended to hold off south of London after they had escorted the bombers in to save fuel (and to avoid the London flak) and met them again on the way out. However, with the RAF soon to go on the offensive and the Jagdgeschwader re-equipping with the Bf 109F, and later the Fw 190, this would become less of a problem over northern France and the Low Countries.

On 10 July 1941, the RAF managed to obtain a pristine example of a Bf 109F. The target that day was Chocques Power Station, north-west of Béthune in northern France by three Stirling bombers from 7 Squadron. These three aircraft had a massive escort of Spitfires and Hurricanes.

South of Boulogne, the first German fighters were seen and both the RAF and Luftwaffe pilots started circling to get in the best position to attack. One of the German fighters was flown by 28-victory ace Hauptmann (Hptm) Rolf Pingel Kommandeur of I./JG 26. He later reported he had chased and attacked the Stirling flown by Plt Off Charles Rolfe. According to Rolfe, they were attacked by a single Me 109 and his bomber received hits in the tail by cannon fire. However, the Stirling's beam gunner reported hitting this aircraft in the engine and claimed it as damaged. Rolf Pingel stated that his engine failed and he was forced to crash-land his Bf 109F-2 at St Margaret's Bay, Dover. Attempts by Pingel to set his aircraft alight were soon deterred by a burst of machine-gun fire over his head.

As the war continued, newer Allied and Soviet fighters forced further developments with further improvements to the Bf 109F and then the introduction to service of the Bf 109G (Gustav) and, ultimately, at the end of the war, the Bf 109K. The Bf 109 served on all fronts with the Luftwaffe and was operated by a number of Germany's allies, namely Bulgaria, Croatia, Hungary and Italy. It was also operated by the Finnish Air Force, Slovak Air Force, Spain, Switzerland and Yugoslavia.

Basic Bf 109 operational variants

Variant	Engine	Basic Armament	Other Changes
B-1	Jumo 210Da (B-2 with Jumo 210 Ea)	2 x MG 17, engine-mounted MG 17 or MG FF	
D	Daimler-Benz 600Aa	"	
E-1	DB 601A	4 x MG 17	E-1/B Jabo
E-3	"	2 x MG17; 2 x MG FF	E-3/B Jabo
E-4	DB 601A or N	2 x MG17; 2 x MG FF/M	E-4/B Jabo. Additional armour and modified cockpit
E-7	"	"	Fitted with 300-litre drop tank
E*	DB 601E	"	
T-1	DB 601N	"	Intended for used on *Graf Zeppelin* carrier
T-2	"	"	As T-1 but carrier equipment removed
F-1	"	2 x MG 17; 1 x MG FF/M	
F-2	"	2 x MG 1; 1 x MG 151/15	
F-4	DB 601E	2 x MG 17; 1 x MG 151/20	
G-1	DB 605A	1 x MG 151/20; 2 x MG 17; possible 2 x underwing MG 151/20	Pressurised cockpit
G-2	"	"	
G-3	"	"	As G-1 but new radio
G-4	"	"	As G-2 but new radio
G-5	"	2 x MG 131; 1 x MG 151	Pressurised cockpit
G-6	"	2 x MG 131; 1 x MG 151; possible underwing 21cm rockets instead of MG 15/20	
G-8	"	2 x MG 131	Recce
G-10	DB 605D	2 x MG 131; 1 x MG 151/20 or MK 108	
G-12	DB 605A	2 x MG 17	Two-seat trainer
G-14	DB 605AM	1 x MG 151/20; 2 x MG 131	
K-4	DB 605D	2 x MG 131/MG 151; 1 x MK 103/108	
K-14	DB 605L	2 x MG 131; 1 x MK 108	Very limited numbers became operational, if any

Right: Bf 109B of J/88, Spain 1938.

Below: Bf 109E-1 of I./Jagdgeschwader I./JG 77.

Bf 109E-4s of I./JG 77, 1940.

Bf 109Es of 5./JG 53, Cherbourg-Ost, August 1940.

Bf 109 F-2 of 9./JG 2, 1941.

Bf 109 G-4 of 1./JG 27, France, 1943.

Above: Bf 109 G-6s of 9./JG 27, Vienna, April 1944.

Right: Bf 109 G-6 of 9./JG 26 about to be shot down, 5 November 1943.

Above: Bf 109 G-6 of III./JG 26, France, June 1944.

Left: Bf 109 G-6 of 5./JG 2, France, 1944.

Below: Bf 109 G-14 of 4./JG 3, November 1944.

Above: The unusual Bf 109 G-12 two-seat trainer.

Right: Bf 109 G-6s captured at Fassberg at the end of the war.

Messerschmitt Bf 110

The Messerschmitt Bf 110 was the Luftwaffe's first long-range fighter and served as a fighter, bomber destroyer, fighter-bomber, reconnaissance aircraft and night-fighter in all theatres for the duration of the war.

In 1934, the RLM issued the requirement for an aircraft capable of escorting bombers deep into enemy territory. It would have twin-engines, three seats, be all metal, be armed with cannon and could carry bombs. Three companies took up the challenge, namely Focke-Wulf, Henschel and Willi Messerschmitt's Bayerische Flugzeugwerk AG (Bf). The Bf 110V1 first flew on 12 May 1936 powered by Junkers Jumo 210 engines, when it was found to be not as manoeuvrable as hoped but faster than expected. A second prototype flew on 24 October 1936 and a third with Daimler-Benz DB 600 engines on 24 December 1936, the latter being armed with four forward-firing MG 17 machine guns and a rear-firing MG 15. Both the Bf 110V2 and V3 were evaluated by the Luftwaffe, and with Bf (subsequently Messerschmitt) omitting an

Bf 110B of II./ZG 141, 1938.

internal bomb bay, which gave it an edge over its competitors, the company was instructed in January 1937 to build seven Bf 110A-0s powered by Junkers Jumo 210B engines for service evaluation. This was followed by the Bf 110B-1, which had an additional two 20mm MG FF cannon fitted under the machine guns. The Jumo 210Gs were still found to be problematic, and two Bf110s were test flown with the DB600 engine (eventually replaced by the DB601 engine), which offered more power and resulted in the first major variant, the BF 110C. This variant had minor modifications to the cockpit and structure but, unlike the Bf 109, it arrived too late to be trialled in Spain. However, it was active from the first day of World War Two in Poland, flying with I./Zerstörergeschwader 1 (I./ZG 1), I. (Zerstörer)/Lehrgeschwader 1 (I.(Z)./LG 1) and I./ZG 76. All three units were equipped with a mix of Bf 110Bs or Cs and although II./ZG 1 and I./ZG 2 also took part in the attack on Poland, they were equipped with Bf 109s but would convert to the Bf 110 when more were available towards the end of the year.

By the start of the Battle of France, Bf 110Cs equipped I. and II./ZG 1, Stab and I./ZG 2, ZG 26, I./ZG 52 (which would become II./ZG 2 at the end of June 1940) and I. and II./ZG 76 (I./ZG 76 would operate over Norway April–June 1940 with its long-range Bf 110D-0/R1s). A number of reconnaissance units would soon be equipped by the Bf 110 by the start of the Battle of Britain.

Bf 110Cs of I./ZG 76, Poland, September 1939.

During the Battle of Britain, the Bf 110 was also used by 1. and 2./Erprobungsgruppe 210 in the fighter-bomber role as well as a number of its Bf 110s being armed with a 30mm cannon. However, despite the audacious attacks by this unit, 28 Bf 110s were lost in the Battle of Britain, with three Gruppen Kommandeurs and one Bf 110 Staffelkapitän being killed.

However, it soon became clear that against more modern fighters, the Bf 110 was vulnerable in daylight, forcing crews to go into a defensive circle for mutual defence. A new role for the Bf 110 was therefore found when, in June 1940, Maj Wolfgang Falck was tasked to form a night-fighter unit for defence of the Reich. The preferred night-fighters were the Bf 110 and Junkers Ju 88C-2/C-4 heavy fighter and to meet the demand, a number of units were re-roled, in part helped by their daytime losses. The first Bf 110 victory then came on 20 July 1940, and by the end of 1940, Bf 110 pilots had claimed 28 aircraft by night.

The year 1941 saw the arrival of the Bf 110F (essentially the same as the E series but powered by DB 601F engines) but by now it was anticipated that the Bf 110 would be replaced by the Me 210. Production of the Bf 110 had already begun to fall in anticipation but the Me 210 was plagued with problems, so it was decided to improve the existing Bf 110 by fitting it with DB 605B engines, and the aircraft became the Bf 110G. The G-2 was the heavy fighter version with the ability to be a Jabo, the G-3 reconnaissance version and the G-4 night-fighter. External armament included a 37mm (G-2/R1) cannon, which could be armed with four 21cm underwing rockets and a 15mm gun pack under the fuselage; the internal armament was also changed, with the 20mm cannon being replaced by the faster firing MG 151 or, in the case of the Bf 110G-2/R4, two 30mm cannon. Twin MG 81s were fitted for rear defensive fire while, in the night-fighter, in addition to radar, some aircraft were fitted with obliquely mounted MG FF cannon known as Schräge Musik. By means of example, a Bf 110 G-4/R3 captured in September 1944 had two MG 151/20s under the fuselage, two MK 108/30s in the nose, two MG FF/20mm Schräge Musik cannons behind the cockpit and two MG 81/7.92mm cannons firing backwards. However, Bf 110s operating in daylight suffered badly against American long-range fighters, while at night, the Bf 110 was easy prey for the de Havilland Mosquito.

Due to the failure of the Me 210, and then the late operational arrival of the Me 410, around 1,580 Bf 110Gs were delivered in 1943, with a similar number in 1944, after which production tailed off dramatically. The Bf 110 also flew with Hungarian, Italian, Romanian and Croatian air forces but in very small numbers, and at the end of the war, many Bf 110s were found abandoned or destroyed across Europe and Russia and, as a result, some still exist. A number of Bf 110s have recently been found in and recovered from Russia in the years since 1945, but the best example on current display is Bf 110G-4/R-6 Werk Nummer (Wk Nr) 730301 coded D5+RL of 3./NJG 3, which is now in the RAF Museum in Hendon. It is fitted with FuG 220 Lichtenstein SN-2 radar and Schräge Musik. On display at the Deutsches Technikmuseum in Berlin is a Bf 110F-2 Trop, Wk Nr 5052 LN+NR of 13.(Z)/JG 5.

Basic Bf 110 operational variants

Variant	Engines	Basic Armament	Other Changes
C-1	DB 601A	4 x MG 17 and 2 x MG FF in nose; 1 x MG 15 firing rear	FuG III radio
C-2	"	"	FuG X radio
C-3	"	4 x MG 17 and 2 x MG FF/M in nose; 1 x MG 15 firing rear	Probably as C-1
C-4	"	"	As C-2
C-5	"	4 x MG 17; 1 x MG 15	Fitment of RB 50/30 camera
C-6	"	4 x MG 17; 1 x 30 mm, 1 x MG 17	Only 12 built
C-7	"	4 x MG 17 and 2 x MG FF/M in nose; 1 x MG 15 firing rear	Fitted with central bomb rack
D-1	"	"	Extended range
D-0/R1	"	"	Fitted with Dackelbauch 1050-litre belly tank and 900-litre wing tanks. Only used by I./ZG 76.
D-2	DB 601A	4 x MG 17 and 2 x MG FF/M in nose; 1 x MG 15 firing rear	Fitted with wing-mounted 300-litre tanks and centre-line bomb rack
D-3	"	"	Lengthened tail. 300-litre or 900-litre wing tanks. ETC500 bomb rack
D-4	"	4 x MG 17; 1 x MG 15 firing rear	Fitted with Rb 50/30 camera for reconnaissance. 300-litre or 900-litre fuel tanks
E-1	DB 601A	4 x MG 17 and 2 x MG FF/M in nose; 1 x MG 15 firing rear	Extended tail, cockpit heating, enlarged wheels, ETC50 bomb racks under wings
E-2	"	"	As E-1. Lengthened tail
E-3	"	4 x MG 17; 1 x MG 15 firing rear	Fitted with Rb 50/30. 300-litre or 900-litre fuel tanks
F-2	"	4 x MG 17 and 2 x MG FF/M in nose; 1 x MG 17 or MG 81Z firing rear	Long-range Zerstörer
F-3	"	4 x MG 17; 1 x MG 15 or MG 81Z firing rear	Fitted with Rb 50/30. 300-litre or 900-litre fuel tanks
F-4	DB 601F	4 x MG 17 and 2 x MG FF/M in nose; 1 x MG 15 or MG 81Z firing rear (F-4/M1 had 2 x MG 151/20)	Three-man night-fighter
G-2	DB 605B	4 x MG 17 and 2 x MG151/20 in nose; 1 x MG 81Z firing rear	Jabo and Zerstörer

Variant	Engines	Basic Armament	Other Changes
G-2/R1	"	4 x MG 17 in nose; BK 3,7 under fuselage	Zerstörer
G-2/R2	"	4 x MG 17; BK 3,7	GM 1 nitrous oxide tank fitted
G-2/R4	"	2 x MK 108, BK 3,7	
G-3	"	4 x MG 17; 1 x MG 81Z firing rear	Reconnaissance
G-4	"	4 x MG 17 and 2 x MG 151/20 in nose; 1 x MG 81Z firing rear	Night-fighter. Could also be fitted with 2 x MG FF/M Schräge Musik.

Right: Working on the guns of a Bf 110C of 1./ZG 76, 1940.

Below: Bf 110D-0/R1 of 1./ZG 76, July 1940.

Above: Bf 110C Jabo, 1940.

Left: Bf 110C-6 with 30mm cannon, 1./Erprobungsgruppe 210, France, summer 1940.

Below: Bf 110Ds of 7./ZG 26, Mediterranean, 1941.

Above: Hptm Walter Ehle of II./Nachtjagdgeschwader 1 (NJG 1), 1941.

Right: Bf 110C of NJG 1, 1940.

Below: Bf 110D of III./NJG 1, 1941.

Above: Bf 110G-4.

Left: Bf 110 G-4 fitted with FuG 212 Lichtenstein airborne radar.

Below: Bf 110G-4 of I./NJG 4.

Heavily armed Bf 110G-2s.

Right: Dangerous skies. Bf 110Gs caught by American fighters in daylight, 1944. The latter photograph is of a Bf 110G-4 fitted with the FuG-220 radar.

Below: Bf 110G-2s equipped with BK 3,7 cannon, Germany 1944.

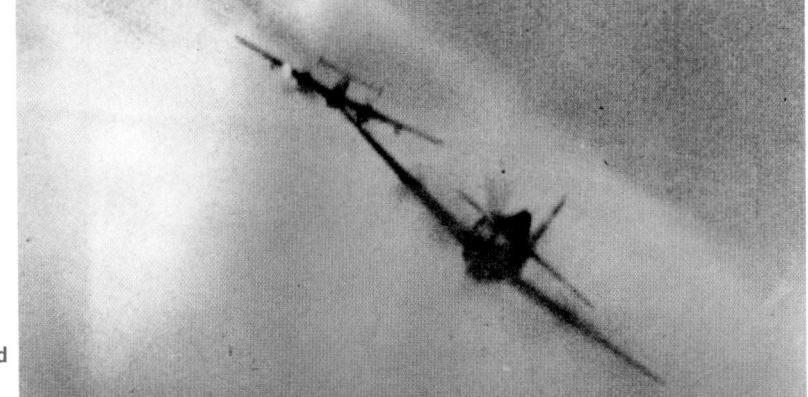

Chapter 2
Sitzkrieg

Although Britain and France declared war on Germany on 3 September 1939, some German fighter units had to wait until 10 May 1940 and the start of the Battle of France for the air war to well and truly start for them. The previous eight months were mainly a sitting and waiting game, which became known by the Germans as Sitzkrieg.

Early days

On 15 March 1937, Jagdgeschwader 334 (JG 334) was formed. Commanded by former World War One ace Oberst Bruno Lörzer, I Gruppe, commanded by Hptm Hubert Merhart von Bernegg, and II Gruppe, commanded by Hptm Hans-Detlev Herhudt von Rohden, were initially based at Mannheim-Sandhofen but Stab and I./JG 334 moved to Wiesbaden-Erbenheim via Frankfurt Rebstock in May 1937.

The Geschwader was initially equipped with the Arado 68 biplane fighter but, early in 1938, began converting to the Bf 109B. It was therefore understandable that quite a number of JG 334 pilots flew as part of the Condor Legion in the Spanish Civil War.

Name	Kills in Spain
Oberleutnant (Oblt) Hubertus von Bonin	1
Leutnant (Lt) Heinz Bretnütz	2
Unteroffizier (Uffz) Günther Freund	2
Lt Rudolf Goy	3
Oberfeldwebel (Ofw) Heinz Grimmling	1
Hptm Harro Harder	11
Uffz Willibald Hien	4
Ofw Fritz Hillmann	3
Hptm Lothar Von Janson	1
Uffz Karl Kolb	1
Uffz Erich Kuhlmann	4
Lt Wolfgang Lippert	5
Oblt Hans-Karl Mayer	8
Oblt Werner Mölders	14
Oblt Rolf Pingel	6
Ofw Ignaz Prestele	4
Uffz Bernhard Seufert	3
Uffz Alfred Stark	1

Other pilots are known to have flown in Spain but did not claim any victories, namely Oblt Ernst Boenigk, Oblt Hubert Kroeck, Oblt Alfred von Lojewski, Oblt Günther Schulze-Blanck, Lt Werner Ursinus and Oblt Wolf-Dietrich Wilcke. Many of these pilots would go on to be successful and highly decorated fighter pilots in World War Two, but few would survive the war.

Bf 109 Es of 1./JG 53 at Wiesbaden Erbenheim at the outbreak of war.

One pilot whose name stands out was Werner Mölders. Born in Gelsenkirchen on 18 March 1913, he joined the German military in 1931 and began training as a pilot in 1934. His first posting as a fighter pilot was to JG 134 and he became the Staffel Kapitän (St Kap) of 1./JG 334 when it was formed. He did not arrive in Spain until the middle of April 1938, after which he took command of the Bf 109-equipped 3./Jagdgruppe 88 (3./J88) from Oblt Adolf Galland. He was another pilot who would become a successful fighter pilot, although he left Spain without a single kill to his name as most of his missions were ground attacks. Mölders scored his first and second kills on 15 July 1938 and by the time he handed over his Staffel to Oblt Hubertus von Bonin at the start of December 1938, he had shot down 14 aircraft, his last being on

Above left: Ofw Walter Grimmling of 1 Staffel, who shot down the Geschwader's first aircraft on 9 September 1939. He would be killed on 14 May 1940.

Above right: Uffz Heinrich Bezner of 1 Staffel, one of four pilots that shot down Mureaux 115s on 10 September 1939. He would be killed 26 August 1940.

Above left: Lt Georg Claus of 1 Staffel would claim a Mureaux on 10 September 1939. He would be killed on 11 November 1940 while flying with JG 51.

Above right: Standing on the far right is Lt Walter Rupp of 1 Staffel (seen here as Oblt commanding 3./JG 53 in September 1940). He claimed an unconfirmed Curtiss P-36 on 24 September 1939.

3 November 1938. Being the top scorer of the Condor Legion, he was awarded the Spanish Cross in Gold with Swords and Diamonds. On his return to Germany, he was posted onto the staff of the Inspekteur der Jagdflieger of the RLM in Berlin, where his current and extensive combat experience as a fighter pilot was put to good use in developing future tactics and techniques.

Meanwhile, JG 334, now commanded by Oberstleutnant (Obstlt) Werner Junck, another World War One fighter pilot, had in November 1938 been re-designated JG 133 (and was formed of just I. and II. Gruppe) and was to re-assume command of 1./JG 133 that Werner 'Vati' Mölders returned in March 1939. His fellow St Kaps were also ex-Condor Legion pilots, namely Oblt Rolf Pingel in 2 Staffel and Hptm Lothar von Janson in 3 Staffel. Shortly after, Von Janson took over command of I. Gruppe and was replaced by Oblt Wolfgang Lippert, another Condor Legion old hand.

II./JG 133 was also commanded by a mix of combat experienced and relatively inexperienced pilots. Hptm Hubert Merhart von Bernegg had moved from being Gruppen Kommandeur (Gr Kdr) of I./JG 334 to II Gruppe the previous year. Ex-Condor Legion pilots Oblt Hubert Kroeck commanded 4 Staffel and Oblt Rudolf Goy commanded 5 Staffel, but 6 Staffel was commanded by Hptm Günther Freiherr von Maltzahn who had not flown in Spain but within five months would replace von Bernegg as II Gr Kdr and his 6 Staffel would now be led by Oblt Heinz Bretnütz, who had flown in Spain.

At the start of May 1939, JG 133 was re-designated JG 53. Now flying the Bf 109E-1 and E-3s, the 'Pik As' (Ace of Spades) Geschwader, as it was soon to be known, was still flying from Wiesbaden-Erbenheim when Germany invaded Poland. Two days later, France and Great Britain declared war on Germany and it would not be long before I. and II./JG 53 were in combat.

Into war

If the Pik As pilots thought they would be immediately in combat with French aircraft, they were wrong. Despite operating in the Saarbrücken/Trier area, which was bordered by neutral Luxembourg and Germany and France, it took some days before anything happened and, when it did, the first casualty was almost Werner Mölders. Some records say that his Bf 109 was damaged in combat by a French Curtiss H-75s of Groupe de Chasse II/4 (GC II/4) on the morning of 8 September 1939, which resulted in him force-landing behind German lines near Birkenfeld. However, despite his logbook confirming he took off from Wiesbaden at 0930hrs on that day on a flight over the front line, it does not mention him meeting any enemy aircraft before he force-landed. Apparently, his aircraft overturned and he suffered minor injuries that kept him off flying until 15 September 1939.

While Mölders was recuperating, his Staffel would score the Geschwader's first kill of the war when former Condor Legion pilot Ofw Heinz Grimmling shot down a Bloch 131 of Groupes Aériennes de Reconnaissance 14 at 1136hrs on 9 September 1939, killing three of its French crew and wounding one. Three hours later, Lt Wilhelm Hoffmann of 3./JG 53 shot down a Bloch 200 believed to be from Groupe de Bombardment I/31, which crashed near Zweibrücken with five

Successful pilots of II Gruppe. Hptm Günther Von Maltzahn (Gr Kdr 68 kills, survived), Oblt Heinz Bretnütz (6 St Kap 32 kills, † 27 Jun 1941), Ofw Werner Kauffmann (4 Staffel 7 kills, † 11 November 1940), Oblt Eduard Schröder (6 Staffel 29 kills, survived), Ofw Albrecht Baun (6 Staffel, 5 kills, † 25 August 1940). Von Maltzahn, Bretnütz, Baun and Schröder would all claim aircraft in September 1939.

crew, including GB I/31's Commandant, Lt Col Enselem, being captured. The following day saw three more kills for 1 Staffel and Oblt Rolf Pingel of 2./JG 53 adding one more to his six kills from Spain. These claims were all for Mureaux high-wing aircraft – all metal monoplanes used for reconnaissance; the French reported the loss of three that day.

20 September 1939 would be a field day for JG 53 and see the first kills for II./JG 53. At 0955hrs, Oblt Heinz Bretnütz of 6./JG 53 was credited with shooting down a balloon and then, two hours later, Lts Albert Richert and Kurt Liedtke of 5 Staffel claimed two Bristol Blenheims near Bitsch. Being the first time that JG 53 had met the RAF, their identification was a bit awry: in fact, they had shot down two Fairey Battles of 88 Sqn that were engaged on a reconnaissance mission. Fg Off Reginald Graveley was one of the pilots and managed to crash-land behind Allied lines. One of his crew was killed and one badly burnt. Graveley, although badly burnt himself, managed to pull his observer from the wreckage to a place of safety, after which he returned to the aircraft to try and recover the body of his gunner, which he was unable to do. Sadly, his observer succumbed to his wounds later that day, but Graveley would be awarded the OBE later that year for his actions to save his crew. The crew of the second Battle, piloted by Flt Sgt Douglas Page, were all killed.

20 September 1939 also saw another four kills for I./JG 53, with all four successful pilots having flown in Spain. Early in the morning, Ofw Ignaz 'Igel' Prestele of 2./JG 53 shot down a balloon, followed three and a half hours later by an unidentified Morane 406 by Ofw Willibald Hein. Mid-afternoon it was the turn of Uffz Günther Freund of 1 Staffel and Werner Mölders, who attacked and shot down two Curtiss H-75s of GC II/5. Sgt Pechaud managed to force-land at St Mihiel without injury to himself, but Sgt Quéguiner, believed to be Mölders' victim, baled out wounded west of Merzig. Mölders' combat report reads as follows:

As the Schwarm [Mölders, Lt Ludwig Brandhuber, Uffz Günther Bleidorn and Uffz Günther Freund] overflew the Saar near Merzig at 4500m, six enemy monoplanes were sighted south of Conz at 5000m. I climbed above the enemy in a wide curve to the north and carried out a surprise attack on the rearmost machine. I opened fire at approximately 50m whereupon the Curtiss began to fishtail. After a further lengthy burst, smoke came out of the machine and pieces flew off it. It then tipped forward into a dive and I lost sight of it.

Other members of Mölders' Schwarm reported seeing the French pilot bale out. With the arrival of winter weather, combats began to decrease, as did the victories. By the end of 1939, I Gruppe had claimed 28 aircraft and two balloons; II Gruppe had claimed 13 aircraft and two balloons. However, one ex-Condor Legion pilot had been killed and another wounded: Ofw Willbald Hein of 3 Staffel was killed in combat on 30 September 1939, just after shooting down his second aircraft of the war, while Oblt Günther 'Schubla' Schulze-Blank of 4 Staffel was wounded in combat the same day. A number of former Condor Legion pilots in I. and II./JG 53 were slowly starting to increase on their scores from Spain, namely Oblt Hans-Karl Mayer (1), Oblt Wolfgang Lippert (1), Oblt Rolf Pingel (2), Ofw Heinz Grimmling (2), Stfw Ignaz Prestele (3), Hptm Lothar Von Janson (1), Oblt Rudolf Goy (1) and Oblt Heinz Bretnütz (2).

One name not on this list was Hptm Werner Mölders who, after just one kill with 1 Staffel, moved to command the newly formed III./JG 53 on 18 September 1939, handing 1 Staffel over to his good friend, Oblt Hans-Karl 'Mayer-Ast' Mayer. By the end of 1939, Mölders had shot down another two aircraft including III Gruppe's first kill, an 18 Sqn Bristol Blenheim flown by Fg Off Denis Elliot, which crashed near Küsserath on 30 October 1939 causing the deaths of its three crew members. By the end of the year, III Gruppe's victories had risen to 10.

It had been a slow but successful start to the war for JG 53, which by now had formally adopted the name 'Pik As', and its

Left: Oblt Heinz Bretnütz of 6./JG 53. He would claim a balloon and one aircraft in September 1939.

Below: Bretnütz's Bf 109 E-4 seen during an exercise in 1940.

aircraft sported an 'ace of spades' badge set in a diamond on either side of their cowlings. 1940 would start as 1939 finished, but with the Sitzkrieg (Phoney War) ending with the start of the Battle of France and then the commencement of the Battle of Britain, JG 53 would see a rapid rise in kills and the emergence of a number of successful pilots, some of whom would not survive the year. Notably, Werner Mölders – who had been promoted to Oberst, awarded the Ritterkreuz with Oakleaves, Swords and Diamonds and become Inspekteur der Jagdflieger having shot down 115 aircraft – was killed in an accident flying as a passenger on 22 November 1941.

Above left: Oblt Hans-Karl Mayer of 1 Staffel. His first kill of 1939 would not be until November.

Above right: Lt Heinz Wittenberg would get two kills during the war with III./JG 53, while Lt Karl-Wilhelm Heimbs of I Gruppe would shoot down two aircraft in September 1939. Heimbs would be killed in action on 30 September 1939.

Above left: I./JG 53 pilots, summer 1940. Oblt Ignaz Prestele (2 Staffel), Lt Karl Leonhard (3 Staffel), Hptm Rolf Pingel (2 Staffel) and Oblt Wolfgang Lippert (3 Staffel).

Above right: Uffz Franz Kaiser of 2 Staffel. He was one of five pilots from his Staffel to shoot down a Fairey Battle on 30 September 1939.

Right: Another successful pilot on 30 September 1939. Uffz Josef Wurmheller would go on to claim 102 kills.

Left: This Bf 109 E-1 of 1 Staffel suffered engine failure on 30 September 1939 and crash-landed near Wiesbaden. The pilot is not known.

Below left: Successful pilots of 3 Staffel on 30 September 1939: Fw Karl Kuhl (far left), Oblt Wolfgang Lippert (second from left) and Ofw Erich Kuhlmann (far right). The pilot second from far right is Lt Julius Haase. Only Kuhl would survive the war; the remainder would all be dead by the end of 1941.

Below right: Werner Mölders' Bf 109 E-4 – proof of his meteoric rise – photographed at the end of May 1940 just before he was awarded the Ritterkreuz. Shortly after, he was shot down and taken prisoner.

Bf 109 Es of JG 53 at Wiesbaden Erbenheim.

Chapter 3
Zerstörer's 11-Month War

The only Messerschmitt Bf 110 flying with Luftflotte 5 in Norway in the Battle of Britain was I Gruppe/Zerstörergeschwader 76 (I./ZG 76) and despite being active and successful over Poland, the North Sea and Norway in the first nine months of the war, its part in the Battle of Britain was very brief.

Busy start

On 1 May 1939, II./ZG 141 became I./ZG 76, moved to Olmütz from Pardubitz and began re-equipping with the Bf 110 from the Bf 109. The Gruppen Kommandeur was Hptm Günther Reinecke with the three Staffelkapitän being Hptm Horst Pape (1 Staffel), Hptm Wolfgang Falck (2 Staffel) and Hptm Josef Gutman (3 Staffel). When, on 1 September 1939, German forces invaded Poland, I./ZG 76, now operating from Ohlau, was involved from the start, escorting bombers attacking Kraków. The following day saw its first combats and losses, with the first victory of the Gruppe going to Lt Heinz Ihrke of 2 Staffel. By the end of that day, nine victories had been claimed but three aircraft from 1./ZG 76 had been shot down or damaged, with two crew members killed.

Between 3 and 11 September 1939, I./ZG 76 claimed another 22 aircraft with the only casualty being Lt Helmut Lent of 1./ZG 76, who became disorientated during a combat mission on 9 September 1939 and force-landed, receiving a bump on the head. At the end of the month, I./ZG 76 returned to Germany but then moved around so that, by the start of December 1939, it was in the Dortmund/Gütersloh area. During this time, command of 1./ZG 76 went to Oblt Werner Hansen.

Fortuitously, on 16 December 1939 and following an armed reconnaissance over the German Bight by Wellingtons of RAF Bomber Command two days before, I./ZG 76 moved to Jever, just south of Wilhelmshaven, and was ideally situated for the unescorted daylight attack on Wilhelmshaven by 24 RAF Wellingtons on 18 December 1939. Exactly half the attacking force was shot down with I./ZG 76 claiming 15 Wellingtons with just Oblt Gustav Uellenbeck of 2./ZG 76 and his radio operator being slightly wounded (and by the same bullet).

Above left: Lt Helmut Lent's crash-landing on 9 September 1939.

Above right: Lt Helmut Lent, who would go on to be Germany's most decorated night-fighter pilot.

For the first three months of 1940, the Gruppe continued to shoot down RAF aircraft, claiming three Wellingtons and three Blenheims in January 1940 and another Blenheim in February 1940. During this time, just one German radio operator was wounded in combat but at least three aircraft were lost in accidents, with three Luftwaffe crew members killed and two injured.

Into the offensive

In the early hours of 9 April 1940, Germany launched Operation *Weserübung*, the attack on Norway and Denmark. The day before, I./ZG 76 had moved to Westerland and the following day, 1./ZG 76 took off, headed for Oslo-Fornebu to provide air support to the airborne forces attacking the airfield. 2./ZG 76 did the same at Aalborg in Denmark and 3./ZG 76 at Stavanger/Sola. Things did not go well for I./ZG 76, neither before nor during the day. Hptm Josef Gutmann, Staffelkapitän of 3./ZG 76, had been killed on 7 April 1940, his Bf 110 hitting a truck on take-off from Jever; he was replaced by Oblt Gordon Gollob. Then, over Stavanger, Bf 110s flown by Lt Sibo Habben and Uffz Gerhard Grams of 3./ZG 76 collided and crashed into the sea; both pilots and their respective radio operators were killed.

For 1./ZG 76, things were slightly better. Uffz Helmut Mütschele was shot down in combat with Norwegian Gloster Gladiators. After crash-landing, he and his radio operator were captured, albeit only briefly. Lt Erhart Kort and his radio operator were also shot down but both were killed. Meanwhile, 1./ZG 76 was strafing the airfield, destroying two Gloster Gladiators; Lt Helmut Lent's aircraft was hit by ground fire and the starboard engine set on fire. At the same time, Oblt Werner Hansen's fighter was also hit and his starboard engine began overheating, so with all his Staffel now low on fuel, Hansen ordered them to land, during which, Lent hit the airfield boundary slope, shearing off the undercarriage – his aircraft ended up on its belly.

By the end of April 1940, 16 more aircraft had been claimed in combat by I./ZG 76 but on 30 April 1940, aircraft flown by Kommandeur Hptm Günther Reinecke and 3./ZG 76's Ofw Georg Fleischmann were both shot down in combat with RAF bombers and, on returning from the same mission, Lt Helmut

Above left: Hptm Günther Reinecke (centre) with two members of his Stab – Lt Heinz Holborn and Oblt Hans Jäger (POW 29 May 1940).

Above right: Distinctive markings on the Bf 110C of Lt Ul Kettling of 1./ZG 76. (left to right): train badge of 1 Staffel, pilot's personal badge and flags of the countries over which he had flown operationally – Czechoslovakia, Poland and Norway.

Fahlbusch of 2./ZG 76 crashed following an engine failure. All six aircrew lost their lives, and command of I./ZG 76 now went to Hptm Werner Restemeyer.

On 18 May 1940, six crews flew to Trondheim to support German operations as part of a Sonderstaffel (special unit) made up of the more experienced pilots from I./ZG 76 who had blind flying experience. The crews would fly the new Bf 110 D-1/R-1, which was fitted with additional ventral and wing-tip fuel tanks for greater range; the wing tanks being the only ones that could be jettisoned. Only one aircraft would be lost in combat during this detachment when, on 29 May 1940, Gruppen Adjutant Oblt Hans Jäger was shot down by Flt Sgt Edward Shacklady of 46 Sqn; Jäger and his radio operator were both captured. I./ZG 76 would continue to operate from Trondheim until mid-July 1940, during which time it would shoot down 22 aircraft. The Battle of Britain was now about to start but would only last one month and five days for I./ZG 76.

Into the battle

Now flying from Stavanger-Forus, the first two victories of the Battle of Britain went to Lt Reinhard Eckardt and Uffz Klaus Ladwein of 2./ZG 76 at 1345hrs on 21 July 1940. That afternoon, a single Hudson of 224 Sqn

Helmut Lent's second crash-landing of the war, Oslo-Fornebu, 9 April 1940.

and three more from 233 Sqn were tasked to attack four minesweepers of 1 Minensuchflottille and the 12,000-ton tanker *Nordmark* west of Haestholm. No German aircraft were reported hit, but one from each squadron failed to return, leading to the deaths of Plt Off Victor Morrison and Plt Off Bill Ather respectively. Then, on 9 August 1940, Klaus Ladwein received his second (and what would be his last) victory of the war when he claimed another Hudson of 224 Sqn flown by Plt Off Roy Forbes, which was on a coastal reconnaissance and was shot down attacking an escort ship in Fedjefjorden near Bergen. All four crew were killed and only the body of Sgt Stephen Grant was recovered and buried at Stavne.

By now, I./ZG 76 had been credited with 99 victories during the war so far and eight days later, it was expected this total would increase. However, disaster was about to befall the Gruppe.

On 15 August 1940, I./ZG 76 with its long-range Bf 110 D-1/R-1s, was tasked to escort Heinkel He 111s of Kampfgeschwader 26 attacking targets in north-east England. Oblt Helmut Lent's logbook says it was his 98th operational flight of the war and that he and radio operator, Uffz Walter Kubisch, took off at 1136hrs and landed at Jever at 1615hrs. In a letter to his parents, he added a little more about what actually happened:

> Recently we were in England. Unfortunately I did not shoot anything down this time. I had a fault with my plane so that I was at a serious disadvantage. In addition, I had a fight with six Spitfires all by myself – a bit much all at one time. Otherwise I got back home OK but once again God the Father mercifully spared me. I landed safely with only a couple of bullet holes. In passing I had a go at two barrage balloons over Hull.

The events of the day are best related by one of the survivors, radio operator Uffz Otto Dombrewsky of 2./ZG 76:

> It was a black day for I./ZG 76. We suffered heavy losses. Our orders: mission against England as protection for He 111s. The Gruppenschwarm with Hptm Werner Restemeyer flew at the rear of the formation in order to intervene wherever the trouble was the greatest but they didn't get the chance. Long before the coast we were surprised by Spitfires and Hurricanes who attacked us in vastly superior numbers. The Gruppenschwarm was the first to be engaged – we could see how they were broken up and Hptm Restemeyer shot down. We had to stay with the bombers and were in turn engaged in battle. Our protective circle was torn open and we were attacked from above and the left by a Hurricane. I shouted my pilot Oblt Gustav Uellenbeck to pull up to the left and was able to open fire at the Hurricane successfully as she dropped away to the left in a steep dive with a trail of smoke. When we got back to Aalborg we counted 24 bullet holes. The direction-finding equipment, aerial – everything had been shot away.

Left: Fitting what was known as the 'Dachshund's Belly' fuel tank.

Below: Tank in place on a Bf 110 of 1./ZG 76.

 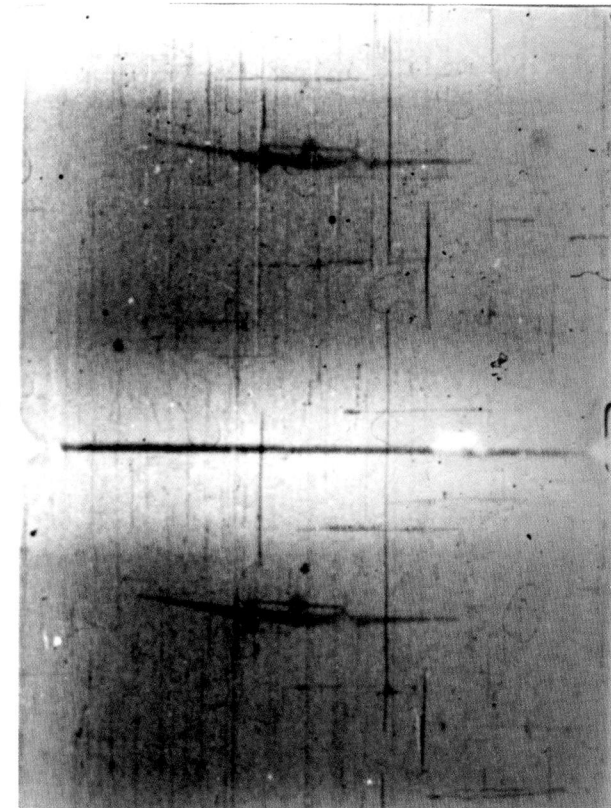

Above left: Lt Hans-Ulrich Kettling of 1./ZG 76.

Above right: Camera gun photograph of Kettling's Bf 110 under attack, 15 August 1940.

The fate of Hptm Restemeyer, his Bordfunker Uffz Werner Eichert and radio specialist Hptm Ernst-August Hartwich is probably best explained by Spitfire pilot Plt Off Desmond Sheen of 72 Sqn:

> I saw what I thought was formation of Ju 88s starting to go into a circle and attacked one of them at close range from dead astern. It either had a large bomb or auxiliary fuel tank underneath. I didn't have time to tell what it was as I must have hit it with my first burst as the whole aircraft literally disintegrated. All that was left was a large black cloud which I had no time to avoid and flew through.

Six Bf 110s were shot down and countless more damaged. In addition to the Gruppen Kommandeur and his crew, Oblt Gustav Loobes, the Gruppen adjutant, and his radio operator were reported missing as well as Lt Heinrich Köhler and his radio operator, and Ofw Hans Gröning and his radio operator, both from 3./ZG 76. In total, 11 aircrew were killed, three were wounded and three were captured. The first two to be captured were Oblt Hans-Ulrich Kettling and his radio operator, Obergefreiter (Ogefr) Fritz Volk, from 1./ZG 76. Ul Kettling recorded what happened:

> About 20 miles from the coast, the first of several waves of Spitfires came in for a fight. Our formation disintegrated into Schwarms, attacking the Spitfires and keeping them away from the bombers. All around, dogfights developed rapidly and I followed my No.1 Oblt Helmut Lent who went after two Spitfires to

protect his rear. I then heard Ogefr Volk working his machine gun and looking back stared into the flaming machine guns of four Spitfires in splendid formation.

Those Spitfires were led by Plt Off Ted Shipman of 41 Sqn, the RAF pilot reporting:

Picking up another Me 110, I tried a series of deflection shots at various ranges with the target wading violently. No result and no return fire. Getting astern of the same target, I tried from about 200yds. This was a long burst and the starboard engine was out of action with clouds of smoke. The Me 110 then made an erratic turn to port and disappeared into the cloud below.

Kettling was forced to shut down the damaged engine only to then be attacked by Plt Off Ben Bennions, also from 41 Sqn, the RAF pilot writing:

I found myself about 300yds astern of an Me 110. I gave him a three second burst and the De Wilde appeared to be striking the fuselage. There was no reply from the rear gunner. The aircraft immediately dived for cloud cover on a south-westerly course. By this time the recoil had put me about 400yds astern but I dived after him closing very slowly. He was travelling very fast indeed and getting closer to the clouds. I gave him another three second burst before entering the clouds.

Ul Ketting recalls what finally happened:

This time they got the port engine, my radio operator and the front windscreen (the bullets missing me by a fraction of inches). Volk was lying on the floor covered in blood and unconscious and I had no means of ascertaining if he was alive or dead so since the flying controls were in perfect order (without the engines of course) and the belly tank empty I decided to bring the plane down for a belly landing.

His Bf 110 finally slithered to a halt at Streatlam near Barnard Castle, where both Germans were quickly captured and where Volk's wounds were found not to be serious. The third German to be captured was the victor of 7 August 1940 – the recently promoted Feldwebel Klaus Ladwein. He was attacked by two

Above left and above right: Kettling's crash-landed fighter near Barnard Castle, 15 August 1940.

Spitfires and, with his two engines hit, he was forced to ditch in the North Sea. He managed to get out but his radio operator, Ogefr Karl Lenk was not so lucky. After being in the sea for four hours, he was picked up by a fishing boat, which later brought him to Edinburgh.

The Gruppe over-optimistically claimed to have shot down 12 RAF fighters that day. Those who claimed were Oblt Werner Hansen (1./ZG 76), Oblt Reinhard Eckardt, Oblt Gustav Uellenbeck, Oblt Helmut Woltersdorf, Ofw Leo Schuhmacher (all from 2./ZG 76) and Oblt Gordon Gollob, Lt Heinrich Köhler, Ofw Hans Gröning, Ofw Lothar Linke and Uffz Erich Zickler (all from 3./ZG 76), with Woltersdorf and Eckardt claiming two Spitfires; it would appear that five of these were unconfirmed. The RAF suffered just four Hurricanes damaged by return fire, two of Ih crash-landed and were written off. However, RAF claims were equally optimistic, with 13 Bf 110s destroyed and one probably destroyed; it also claimed to have shot down five Ju 88s, probably destroyed another three, destroyed a Do 215 and probably destroyed a Do 17 plus another two damaged. There were no Ju 88s, Do 215s or Do 17s taking part in this attack.

This was the end of I./ZG 76 as a day fighter unit. On the evening of 29 August 1940, Helmut Lent recorded in his logbook that he flew from Stavanger to Achmer in Germany and then on 2 September 1940 from Achmer to Lechfeld where, two days later, he and the survivors of his Gruppe started retraining as a night-fighter Gruppe. Many of those who survived 15 August 1940 would later go on to become successful night-fighter pilots – Oblt Reinhard Eckardt, Ofw Lothar Linke, Ofw Herbert Schob and Ofw Leo Schumacher would all be awarded the Ritterkreuz, while Oblt Gordon Gollob (who converted to day fighters) and Oblt Helmut Lent would be awarded Germany's highest award: the Ritterkreuz with Oakleaves, Swords and Diamonds (Lent's radio operator, Uffz Walter Kubisch, would also receive the Ritterkreuz). However, only Schob, Schumacher and Gollob would survive the war.

It had been a short but brutal war for the Bf 110 crews from I./ZG 76, a war which lasted two weeks short of a year. In human terms, in just under 12 months, 29 aircrew were killed, five were captured and 12 suffered varying degrees of injuries or wounds. However, for those who survived its final day of combat, the war would now be different and much longer, and few would live to see its end.

Chapter 4

Butcher Bird

A German fighter which made an immediate impact when it first appeared over the Channel in the summer of 1941 was the Focke-Wulf Fw 190. It totally outclassed the current versions of Spitfire and Hurricane, causing some degree of concern within the RAF – concern that was well founded from the outset.

Design and development

In late 1937, the RLM placed a development contract with the Focke-Wulf Flugzeugbau GmbH for a new single-seat fighter that would eventually replace the Messerschmitt 109. A series of design proposals were submitted to the RLM, most of which included the aircraft being powered by a liquid-cooled inline engine. However, Dipl. Ing. Kurt Tank, Focke-Wulf's technical director, proposed the aircraft be powered by an air-cooled radial engine using the powerful BMW 139. Kurt Tank successfully persuaded the RLM which, in 1938, issued a contract for three prototypes of what would be called the Fw 190. In keeping with tradition, Focke-Wulf also gave the aircraft the name of a bird of prey, in this case Würger ('Butcher Bird' or 'Shrike').

The first prototype, the Fw 190V1 coded D-OPZE, featured a ducted spinner and first flew from the Neuenlander Feld on 1 June 1939, with Flugkapitän Hans Sander, Focke-Wulf's chief test pilot, at the controls. Apart from minor technical concerns, the aircraft proved to have excellent manoeuvrability, good control response, a high rate of roll and a good diving speed. However, the BMW 139 was prone

The first prototype showing its ducted spinner.

Butcher Birds rolling off the production line at Bremen.

to overheating, even with the ducted spinner removed, so it was decided to fit the fifth prototype with the better, albeit bigger and heavier, BMW 801. As a result, airframe changes were made that included a smaller wing (designated V5k) and a larger wing (V5g). While testing continued, construction of 40 pre-production aircraft (the A-0) began and, in March 1941, six aircraft were assigned to the Erprobungsstaffel 190, the unit responsible for operationally testing the Fw 190, at Rechlin-Roggenthin. This unit was essentially made up from elements of II Gruppe./Jagdgeschwader 26 (II./JG 26) and was commanded by experienced pilot Oblt Otto Behrens.

Into action

The Fw 190A-1 would now be tested under operational conditions. It was armed with four MG 17s (two on the front fuselage and two in the wing roots), with two 20mm MG FF cannon fitted outboard on the wing. This was quickly followed by the A-2, which saw the two inboard MG 17 machine guns replaced with two MG FF cannon. However, the BMW 801C engine still suffered from overheating and the cannon's slow firing. Changes made to combat this resulted in the A-3, which featured an BMW 801D engine, an outboard MG FF cannon the improved 20mm MG 151 fitted in the inboard positions.

In July 1941, Erprobungsstaffel 190 moved from Rechlin to Le Bourget near Paris and began converting II./JG 26, commanded by Hptm Walter Adolph, to the Fw 190. By the start of September 1941, all of II Gruppe had converted but it is believed that the first combat took place in the early morning of 16 August 1941 when Hptm Adolph led a mixed Fw 190/Bf 109 formation that claimed to have shot down four Spitfires. The first Fw 190 to be lost was on 21 August 1941 when Ofw Walter Meyer of 6./JG 26

Early Fw 190A-1s seen at Bremen, spring 1941.

suffered an engine failure and then, on 29 August 1941, Lt Heinz Schenk, also from 6 Staffel, was shot down and killed by German flak.

RAF pilots soon reported encountering radial-engined fighters over France, thinking they were ex-French Air Force Curtiss Hawk 75s, but as one RAF pilot noted, 'No Hawk ever had the performance of that brute!' They soon realised they were up against the Fw 190.

As 1941 progressed, the remaining Gruppe from JG 26 converted to the Fw 190, followed in 1942 by JG 2. RAF pilots were finding how inferior their fighters now were, especially when the Fw 190 was flown by an experienced pilot. However, with the Fw 190 still operating over Europe and the Channel, the RAF still knew little about the intricacies of this German fighter. Despite this, on 18 September 1941, 24 victory ace Hptm Walter Adolph was scrambled in his Fw 190A-1 to intercept RAF aircraft off the Belgian coast but failed to return; he had become the pilot of the first Fw 190 to be shot down, the successful pilot being Plt Off Cyril Babbage of 41 Sqn. However, the mysteries of the Fw 190 would all change on 23 June 1942.

Early that evening, six Douglas Bostons of 107 Sqn took off from RAF Exeter to attack a target at Morlaix in Brittany, the escort being provided by Spitfires of the Perranporth and Exeter Wings. At Cherbourg-Maupertus, Fw 190s of III./JG 2 were scrambled and followed the RAF back to the Devon coast where they pounced. One Fw 190 collided with the Exeter wing leader, the German pilot, Uffz Willi Reuschling of 7./JG 2, baling out to be captured, while Wg Cdr Alois Vasatko was killed. A series of dogfights then ensued with the RAF coming off worse. Oblt Armin Faber of Stab III./JG 2 shot down a Spitfire of 310 Sqn and probably damaged another from 19 Sqn, after which he apparently became

Above left: The Fw 190A-3 of III./JG 2, which landed in error at RAF Pembrey, 23 June 1942.

Above right: Fw 190A-3 coded White 6+I of 7./JG 2. This aircraft was flown regularly by Uffz Otto Kleinert.

Above: Fw 190A-5/U8.

Right: Fw 190A-4 Jabo of 10./JG 26, France, 1943.

disorientated and landed his Fw 190A-3 at RAF Pembrey in South Wales, presenting the RAF with a pristine Fw 190, which would be comprehensively evaluated.

Jabo

The Fw 190 also proved itself to be an ideal fighter-bomber. Fitting bombs to German fighters had started in the Battle of Britain but, by 1941, interest in Jagdbomber or Jabo (fighter-bomber) missions had become secondary, and only against shipping. However, Oblt Frank Liesendahl of JG 2 convinced the Luftwaffe to form a dedicated Jabostaffel, flying the Bf 109F. Liesendahl experienced success to such an extent that, in March 1942, the Jabostaffel became 10.(Jabo)/JG 2, and JG 26 was ordered to form its own 10 Staffel. Then, in June 1942, both Jabostaffel moved to Le Bourget to convert to the Fw 190. This was worrying for the RAF as the Fw 190 had already proven itself superior in all flight parameters (apart from turning radius) to the Spitfire Mark Vb, being 30mph faster and having the highest rate of roll of any World War Two fighter. It could also carry a single 500kg bomb under the fuselage and four 50kg bombs under the wings – twice the bomb load of a Bf 109F.

The British now increased their fighter, balloon and gun defences, but Jabo attacks continued from east to west across southern England. A new Fw 190-equipped Jabo unit, Schnellkampfgeschwader 10 (SKG 10), became operational at the start of March 1943, after which it subsumed 10./JG 2 and 10./JG 26. With nearly 120 Jabos available by mid-April 1943, it came as a great surprise to both the Luftwaffe pilots and the RAF that following II. and IV./SKG 10 joining III./SKG 10 in the Mediterranean in June 1943, I./SKG 10 was then used solely for nocturnal attacks and, as a result, the last daylight attacks came on 6 June 1943.

The first nocturnal attack by SKG 10 on the night of 16 April 1943 was a farce. Two aircraft were lost in accidents during the day, with one pilot killed. Then three Fw 190s collided taking off for the mission, with one pilot killed, while two more suffered take-off accidents. Over Britain, four pilots became disorientated, with one being killed when his aircraft ran out of fuel; the remaining three landed or tried to land at a British airfield. A final pilot disappeared – the total cost for the night being ten aircraft destroyed, two damaged, four pilots killed and three captured. Nevertheless, such Jabo night missions continued until June 1944, after which they carried on over mainland Europe.

Final designs

As the war continued and the threat evolved, newer variants of the Fw 190 emerged. The Fw 190F was designed as a Jabo, while the Fw 190G was designed to carry more ordnance to attack mass bomber formations and ground targets. The Fw 190D (or more commonly known as Dora 9) was an attempt to reassert the Fw 190 as a first-rate fighter aircraft. With its long nose (as Allied pilots would also describe it), it would become the fastest fully operational piston-engined fighter of the war, and the D-9 would ultimately become the Ta 152 but too late to make a difference. Like the Bf 109, the Fw 190 served on all fronts with the Luftwaffe.

Very few other countries operated the Fw 190 in World War Two. Germany's ally Hungary was the main operator, while 72 Fw 190A-3s were exported to Turkey between July 1942 and March 1943. Volunteers from the Spanish Air Force operated a number over the Eastern Front, while Romania, which stopped supporting Germany in August 1944, captured a number of Fw 190s, which were apparently not used operationally.

Fw 190 operational variants

Variant	Engine	Armament	Other Changes
A-1	BMW 801C-1	4 x MG 17 2 x MG FF	
A-2	BMW 801C-2	2 x MG 17, 2 x MG 151/20, 2 x MG FF	As A-1; wingspan increased
A-3	BMW 801D-2	"	As A-2
A-4	"	"	Radio upgrade, supplementary fuel injection system
A-5	"	"	Lengthened fuselage due to redesigned engine mounting, application of Umbau Rüstsätze such as cameras

Variant	Engine	Armament	Other Changes
A-6	"	2 x MG 17, 4 x MG 151/20	Modified wing & armament, application of Umbau Rüstsätze
A-7	"	2 x MG 131 4 x MG 151/20	As A-6
A-8	"	2 x MG 131 4 x MG 151/20 optionally 2 x MG 131 2 MG 151/20 2 MK 108	Radio upgrade, repositioned bomb rack
D-9	Jumo 213 A	2 x MG 131 2 x MG 151/20	
F-1	BMW 801D-2	2 x MG 17 2 x MG 151/20	Jabo based on A-4
F-2	"	"	Jabo based on A-5. Improved canopy
F-3	"	"	Jabo based on A-6
F-8	"	2 x MG 131, 2 x MG 151/20	Jabo based on A-8
F-9	BMW 801TS	"	Jabo
G-1	BMW 801D-2	2 x MG 151/20	Long range Jabo based on A-4
G-2	"	"	As G-1 based on A-5
G-3	"	"	As G-2 with auto-pilot PKS 11
G-8	"	"	As G-2 based on A-8

Above left: Fw 190A-3/U7 was produced with a BMW 801C engine, carburettor air intakes outside and fuselage guns removed; it was used as a high-altitude fighter (Höhenjäger).

Above right: From November 1942 to March 1943, II./JG 2 operated in the Mediterranean.

Right: Fw 190A-5s of the reconnaissance unit 2./Nahaufklärungsgruppe 13 seen at Cuers-Pierrefeu, near Toulon, in 1944. The fairing for the cameras is just visible underneath the fuselage, below the numeral.

Above: Fw 190F-8 of I./Schlachtgeschwader 2, Hungary, January 1945.

Left: This is believed to be Fw 190A-6, Werk Nummer 550803 Black 4 of 5./JG 1, which was shot down by a P-47 on 11 November 1943 and crashed at Limbergen, northeast of Dülmen, killing its pilot Unteroffizier Erwin Wessely.

Below left: An Fw 190A-8/R2 of 8./JG 300, December 1944.

Below right: An Fw 190 D-9 seen at Bremen, September 1944.

Chapter 5
Fighter-Bombers Over Dieppe

19 August 1942 saw Allied troops attempting a raid on Dieppe. Luftwaffe aircraft were in action quite quickly. However, for one unit, the day was particularly successful, if not dramatic.

Scramble

For Jabo (fighter-bomber) pilot Lt Leopold Wenger of the Fw 190 equipped 10 (Jabo) Staffel/Jagdgeschwader 2 (10./JG 2,) he and the other pilots of his Staffel were asleep in their billets near Caen when news of the Dieppe raid came through and he and two other pilots were quickly ordered to carry out an armed reconnaissance. However, what happened on take-off he had reason to remember well:

> I had lousy luck and at the same time a lot of good luck. Whilst opening the throttle, the undercarriage collapsed and I slid along the grass on my 500kg bomb. It was not a very cheering experience, especially when you know about the explosive effect of the bomb or when you have been able to watch its effect during an attack. So I missed the first mission. With a Messerschmitt 108, I then flew from Caen to Ste André to get a new Fw 190 and then flew back to Caen again. Valuable time was lost and I was afraid that I would be too late and the whole fuss would be over!

The two other pilots managed to attack an unidentified warship, but one Focke-Wulf 190 suffered flak damage, while damage caused to the other resulted in a forced-landing to the west of Dieppe.

Shortly afterwards, 10./JG 2 carried out another, this time flown by Oblt Fritz Schröter, Lt Erhard Nippa and Lt Gerhard Limberg, and three hits were reported on another unknown ship. Schröter had recently taken command of the Staffel following the death in action of Hptm Frank Liesendahl on 17 July 1972. Then, at 1033hrs, Wenger and three unidentified NCO pilots took off, each armed with a 500kg bomb:

> When we arrived over Dieppe, the fighting zone was shrouded in mist, dust and dense smoke. The fleet was completely hidden. Everywhere there were muzzle flashes and ashore you could see lots of fires

Above left: Fw 190 A-3 flown by Lt Leopold Wenger; the bomb rack is clearly visible under the fuselage.

Above right: A 250kg bomb about to be loaded onto a 10./JG 2 Jabo.

Above: An early accident suffered by Lt Wenger. His Fw 190A-2 is see here at St André, 31 July 1942.

Left: Taking survivors off the *Berkeley*, 19 August 1942.

from shot down aircraft and burnt-out tanks which had hardly advanced more than 20m up the beach. In the sea, many aircrew were floating in their rubber dinghies.

At exactly midday, we began a low-level attack. At the same moment, a German bomber dived past us into the sea. We advanced in the mist and got to the cause of the smoke screen. All our guns were fired and the bombs released at the same time. A bomb went off under the stern of a destroyer but then I was shot at by all kinds of Flak and because of the fireworks, I couldn't watch any more. The three other Fw 190s flying with me damaged a few more ships and one shot down a Spitfire. Still flying at low level, we fired into the packed landing craft. The effect was devastating.

Destroyer target

10./JG 2 returned virtually unscathed, but it was the next attack, witnessed by Gp Capt Harry Broadhurst DSO DFC AFC, that was the most spectacular and successful. 'Broadie' was Deputy Senior Air Staff Officer at HQ 11 Gp and flew four sorties that day. He took off from Hornchurch at 1230hrs on his third mission, together with Wg Cdr Robin Powell, and recorded the following:

The withdrawal was almost complete and with the exception of a few ships two or three miles off Dieppe, which included the destroyer *Berkeley*, the convoy was in full progress back towards the English coast. After cruising around for a few minutes, Wg Cdr Powell separated from me and went down to sea-level to see the situation from low altitude whilst I circled the Dieppe area gradually losing height down to 18,000ft. I noticed one or two attacks by Do 217s whose bombing appeared to be extremely inaccurate, many of them jettisoning their bombs as soon as they were attacked by Spitfires.

I noticed that the rear of the convoy i.e. that part of it nearest to the French coast was being subjected to the most severe attacks and latterly the majority of these were being directed against the destroyer *Berkeley* which was apparently in difficulties. I called up Hornchurch Control and asked them to suggest to Group Operations that the patrols be concentrated over that area, at the same time calling up the ship control and suggesting that he moved the bottom cover squadron to the immediate vicinity of the *Berkeley*. The ship controller was continuously reporting the presence of Do 217s but I noticed that there were several Fw 190s about, some of them carrying bombs.

Towards the end of my patrol I saw two Focke-Wulfs dive towards the *Berkeley*. I dived after them but could not intercept them until after they had dropped their bombs, one of which appeared to score a direct hit on the stern of the *Berkeley*. I closed in to the rear of the Focke-Wulf as he pulled away from his dive and emptied most of my cannon and machine-gun ammunition into him with good effect.

Four Fw 190s of 10./JG 2 had taken off at 1250hrs, led by Oblt Fritz Schröter. With him was Leopold Wenger and two unnamed NCO pilots. Again, Wenger's recollections were vivid:

The English were withdrawing everywhere but the smoke screen did not help them much. I attacked a second destroyer and achieved a direct hit amidships with an SC500 bomb. During the attack, I was under heavy anti-aircraft fire from the destroyer but when the bomb went off, the guns stopped shooting. An explosion followed-simply disastrous. The whole ship was enveloped in black cloud but then I was chased and attacked by many Spitfires and unfortunately could not watch the complete sinking. In the course of this I had got a good thrashing from the Flak-wing, engine, cowling, undercarriage and tail unit were riddled with bullets. There were also two hits in the cockpit but three had ricocheted off the head armour plate. Of course the mission was worth it.

HMS *Albrighton* sinks the *Berkeley*.

The Type I Hunt-Class destroyer HMS *Berkeley*, commanded by Lt James Yorke RN, had been in almost constant action since the start of the raid, bombarding the town and surrounding cliffs and laying smoke screens. In addition to its normal ship's complement of 146, she was also carrying a number of RAF, Army and United States Army Air Forces (USAAF) observers and air controllers, the senior of which were Lt Col Loren Hillsinger USAAF and Wg Cdr Stanley Skinner. Ordinary Seaman Dick Venables relates what happened:

> All I heard through the headphones was 'aircraft approaching!'; the next thing was an enormous cracking sound, the ship lifted up and we were flung in the air, my contact with the Director Control Tower was broken and I suffered a cut chin from the headset.
>
> When we gathered our senses there was smoke and dust everywhere and we were in complete darkness. The ship had assumed a distinct bows down attitude and we thought she was going to drive herself under as we were still underway. Our natural instincts drove us aft towards the hatchway to the upper deck but on arriving, we found the ladder had disappeared! Fear enhances the adrenalin and I jumped up and managed to get my hands over the edge of the hatch, my two colleagues helped push me up and over. I then pulled them up in turn and we proceeded to the upper deck with great relief!

Another who survived was Supply Assistant Tom Hare:

> For something like six hours that raid lasted, the *Berkeley* was constantly engaged in supporting the landings and running the gauntlet of the Luftwaffe and German shore batteries. Eventually when it was decided that there was no point in continuing the action, the order was given to all participants for the general withdrawal. *Berkeley* together with other ships waited off shore for the last of the evacuees and was constantly under attack. The ship stopped momentarily to pick up from a landing craft a party of Canadian soldiers; many were badly wounded and all were suffering from shock and exhaustion. We made the walking wounded as comfortable as possible and handed round cigarettes and when this was accomplished, I grabbed a tea urn and made my way to the galley to make tea for them. It was just as I got into the galley and had turned on the tap of a large hot water tank that a bomb struck the ship just forward of the bridge, breaking its back. The blast from the bomb broke through the bulkhead and I was enveloped in boiling water. The cooking range on the opposite side of the galley disintegrated and I found myself on the deck of the galley amongst red hot metal. I eventually picked myself up in some pain from the scalds and burns and made my way to the upper deck.
>
> I didn't realise it at the time but I understand that the *Berkeley* was going at full speed when she was hit and with the steering smashed, she continued to sail at high speed in a circle, keeling over so steeply that some of the crew were thrown off her decks.
>
> Just as I reached the upper deck, the 'Abandon ship!' call was made and painfully I made my way to the Carley Float which was my 'abandon ship' post but the float was completely entangled in the broken structure of the bridge where it had been attached. The bombing of the ship had happened in the final moments of the evacuation and my first thoughts were now that there may not be any craft left to come to our rescue but fortunately Steam Gun Boat 8 had witnessed the bombing and quickly returned to pick up the survivors. Unfortunately all of the Canadian soldiers in the forward mess deck and 15 of the ship's company were lost in the bombing. Incidentally, we had picked up a German airman earlier that day and I vividly remember that after the 'abandon ship' was sounded, someone recalled that he was still locked away and a rating was sent to release him.

Aftermath

In addition to the 17 who were killed, the senior of which was Sub Lt Arthur Flory, who had transferred from Motor Launch 291, an unknown number of Canadian soldiers were killed together with Wg Cdr Stanley Skinner. Skinner was a Battle of Britain pilot who had flown night fighters with 604 Sqn. Lt Col Lorin Hillsinger would lose a limb but managed to get into Steam Gun Boat 8. He would be awarded the Distinguished Service Cross for remaining at his post as long as possible and continuing to direct aircraft; he would return to operational flying in 1943. The German airman came from either 5./KG 2 or 9./KG 2. Mortally damaged and with all the survivors and bodies taken off, HMS *Albrighton* was instructed to sink the *Berkeley* which it did with two torpedoes. The second torpedo hit the forward magazine and, following an immense explosion at 1338hrs, just 20 minutes after the German attack, the *Berkeley* sank.

By mid-afternoon, the major battles around Dieppe were over. One further Jabo attack is known to have taken place that day when 10./JG 2 sent five aircraft to attack the retreating ships. Again, Wenger, led the attack:

At 1608hrs, took off again on my third sortie against the fleeing fleet. Eventually we reached a force of big landing craft off Brighton. As a defensive measure there were barrage balloons. We attacked at once and after receiving hits, two ships sank immediately. Unfortunately my bomb went over the ship and exploded 10m besides it but I then shot at it and set fire to the superstructure to make up for it!

With that, the combat at Dieppe ended for us. Our Staffel had sent to the bottom two destroyers, two big landing craft, two escort ships and in addition a Spitfire. It had also damaged one destroyer, one cargo ship, one landing ship and two escort ships.

Oblt Fritz Schröter, Lt Erhard Nippa and Lt Leopold Wenger would all receive the Ritterkreuz, as would Hptm Frank Liesendahl posthumously. Wenger would be killed in action a month before the end of the war, while Lt Gerhard Limberg would be awarded the Deutsches Kreuz in Gold and, after the war, became the Inspector of the Bundesluftwaffe with the rank of Generalleutnant from 1974 to 1978.

Above left: **Pilots of 10./JG 2 photographed on 9 July 1942: Oblt Fritz Schröter (far left), Lt Gerhard Limberg (second from left), Lt Poldi Wenger (third from left), Lt Erhard Nippa (far right). Third from right is Hptm Frank Liesendahl, who would be killed in action eight days after this photograph was taken.**

Above right: **Lt Leopold Wenger (third from left) with his Staffel, Caen, May 1943.**

Chapter 6
Stopgap Night-Fighters

As the night air war over north-west Europe intensified, the Luftwaffe needed more night-fighters. One solution was converting three types of Dornier bombers to fighters – a stopgap measure and far from ideal.

Do 17Z-7 and Z-10

In June 1940, Maj Wolfgang Falck, formerly of 2 Staffel/Zerstörergeschwader 76 (2./ZG 76) and latterly commander of I./ZG 1 was tasked to form a night-fighter unit for defence of the Reich. The preferred night fighters were the Bf 110 and Ju 88C-2/C-4, but there would also be two versions of the Do 17 used as night-fighters: the Z-7 Kauz I and the Z-10 Kauz II (*Kauz* translated as 'Screech Owl'). The glazed nose was removed from a Do 17Z-3 and replaced with the nose from a Ju 88C-2/C-4. The armament was three 7.9mm machine guns and one 20mm cannon and the aircraft was designated the Do 17Z-7. This was soon found to be unsatisfactory and an entirely new nose was designed, which increased the armament to four machine guns and two cannon. In the tip of the nose was an infrared spotlight called Spanner-Anlage, which was later replaced by a first-generation FuG 202 Lichtenstein airborne interception radar. This aircraft was now designated the Do 17Z-10.

Precise numbers of Do 17Z-7 and Z-10s are hard to assess but it is thought that eight Z-7s were produced and the survivors were later converted into Z-10s, of which around 11 were produced. The Z-7 first entered service with I./Nachtjagdgeschwader 1 (I./NJG 1) on or around 22 June 1940, and the first recorded combat probably took place in the early hours of 29 June 1940 when a 58 Sqn Whitley reported damaging a night-fighter near Eindhoven. A Do 17Z-7 of 1./NJG 1 flown by Uffz Hugo Schwarz was damaged in combat and later crash-landed near Mönchengladbach-Schwarz; the pilot and his radio operator were both injured, while the flight engineer later died of his wounds.

Above left: Do 17Z-7 of 2./NJG 2 after being damaged by flak, 9 November 1940.

Above right: Do 17Z-7 of 2./NJG 2.

Above left: Do 17Z-10 of 5./NJG 1 (later 2./NJG 2) with Spanner spotlight in the nose and the scope in the cockpit

Above right: Do 17Z-10 clearly showing the Spanner and its armament.

In August 1940, the Do 17Z-7s and Z-10s became part of II./NJG 1. The Gruppe would be commanded by Maj Karl-Heinrich Heyse and just 5 Staffel, commanded by Hptm Rolf Jung, appears to have operated the Do 17Z-7/Z-10.

On 17 July 1940, Oberst Josef Kammhuber was given command of the new 1 Nachtjagddivision. He firmly believed that suitably converted bombers such as the Do 17Z and Ju 88 flown by experienced crews would be ideal for Fernnachtjagd (long-range night-fighter) missions over the UK. He later said: 'When I want to kill wasps, I smoke out their nest. I don't swat insects in the air one at a time, I go to the nest when they are in!'

So it was that II./NJG 1 and then I./NJG 2 began intruder operations over British airfields from Gilze-Rijen in Holland.

It is difficult to tie the majority of 2./NJG 2's kills to the Kauz II as it was only used in very small numbers and was quickly replaced by the Ju 88C. For example, during the period from June to October 1940, Do 17Z-7s and Z-10s were only used on 19 nights, flying 22 sorties.

However, the first recorded successful interception by a Do 17Z-10 came on the night of 9 September 1940 and was the first success of the war for Fw Hermann Sommer of 5./NJG 1 albeit his claim to have shot down a Blenheim in the circuit at RAF Waddington in Lincolnshire was optimistic. It is believed that Sommer attacked a 15 Sqn Blenheim, which reported being attacked by an enemy aircraft, but the pilot successfully landed the damaged aircraft at RAF Wyton.

The first confirmed kill by a Do 17Z-10 came on 16 October 1940 and was credited to Lt Ludwig Becker of 4./NJG, which was still operating the Do 17Z-10 before converting to the Bf 110 shortly afterwards. Becker shot down a 311 Sqn Wellington engaged in an attack on Kiel. Plt Off Bohumil Landa and three of his crew were killed when the bomber crashed at Oosterwolde in Holland, and two more crew members were captured.

The first confirmed intruder success, almost definitely caused by a Do 17Z-10, was a Hampden shot down by Lt Heinz Völker on 28 October 1940. The 49 Sqn operations record book (ORB) states what happened:

'One aircraft was attacked by an enemy aircraft while circling the Q site on return. The aircraft suffered slight damage including three burst tyres and shot accumulator. Hampden X3027 landed in the sea half a mile off Skegness. It is believed that they had been shot up by an enemy aircraft while over this aerodrome [Scampton]'.

The damaged Hampden landed without incident but there were no survivors from Plt Off John Bufton's aircraft. Völker would then claim a Blenheim over the North Sea on the night of 22 December 1940, again probably flying a Do 17Z-10 but this cannot be matched with any RAF losses. In 1941, Völker would convert to the Ju 88C-2/C-4 and fly with 3./NJG 2, claiming another five RAF aircraft on intruder missions and becoming one of the most successful intruder pilots. There would be one more claim for him when, on 22 July 1941, he collided with a Wellington from 11 Operational Training Unit (OTU) ,which was preparing to land at RAF Bassingbourne; both aircraft then crashed, causing the deaths of the three German and eight RAF aircrew.

There are only three other nights when Luftwaffe records specifically mention Do 17Z-10s shooting down RAF aircraft. The first was the night of 10 February 1941 and was made by Oblt Albert Schulz, whose claim was optimistic and no losses can be attributed to his attack. Furthermore, he actually attacked RAF Coltishall, where 222 Sqn Spitfires and 255 Sqn Hurricanes were carrying out night flying practice.

Hptm Rolf Jung was the next to claim and reported shooting down a Wellington. The only loss that can be attributed was a Wellington from 115 Sqn, which was returning from an attack on Hannover. The pilot managed to crash-land near Swaffham in Norfolk, with just the rear gunner suffering injuries.

On the night of 7 April 1941, Lt Johannes Feuerbaum claimed a Hudson while flying a Do 17Z. On the way home, Feuerbaum then claimed what he thought was a Hereford but was probably a Whitley of 51 Sqn, which reported being attacked by a German aircraft 60 miles east of Flamborough Head.

The final kill that can be attributed to a Do 17Z-10 intruder went to Fw Vincenz Giessübel, who shot dowI 11 OTU Wellington over RAF Bassingbourne on 24 April 1941, which then crashed into and destroyed a second Wellington.

Do 17Z-10 losses were understandably light due to the small numbers involved and because, around 13 October 1941, intruder missions ceased by order of the Führer, who wanted to see RAF bombers burning on German territory rather than British airfields. The first loss came exactly a year earlier when a Do 17Z-10 crashed on landing at Gilze-Rijen, injuring Uffz Erich Götz and two crew members. Then, on 9 November 1940, Ofw Herbert Schmid's Do 17 Z-7 was damaged on an intruder sortie and also crash-landed at Gilze-Rijen. On 5 February 1941, Oblt Otto Hauser's Z-10 went missing on an intruder sortie, and the last loss in combat came on 8 May 1941, when Fw Wilhelm Lettenmeier's Do 17Z-10 was shot down by a 25 Sqn Beaufighter flown by Plt Off David Thompson. The Do 17 crashed at Carrington in Lincolnshire. Lettenmeier was killed and the remaining two crew members were captured.

Although the Do 17Z-10 soldiered on, it was soon replaced by more adept night-fighters, namely the Bf 110, the Ju 88C-4 and even the Do 215B-5. The last recorded incident involving a Do 17Z-10 came on 19 September 1941 when an aircraft of 2./NJG 2 suffered an undercarriage collapse at Gilze-Rijen.

Dornier Do 215B

Dornier had been developing the twin DB 601-engined Do 215 primarily for export, but as early as 23 September 1940, it was proposed that to convert a Do 215B-4 into a night-fighter, it would only need a Kauz II nose fitted, a strengthened fuselage, fitting of additional radios, fitting of guns, removal of cockpit defensive guns, additional armour plating, a gun sight and a reduced crew size of three. The first conversion was expected to be delivered to the Luftwaffe for operational trials at the start of November 1940, but it had been decided that priority would be given for the Do 215 to be operated as a reconnaissance aircraft and, as a result, it appears only 17 aircraft were converted to Do 215B-5 night-fighters, which were given the name Kauz III.

By May 1941, five Do 215s had been delivered to Oblt Hans Röderer's 4./NJG 1. The first record of a Do 215B-5 with II./NJG 1 had come on 15 February 1941 when one was damaged in a ground

Do 215B-5, with both Spanner and FuG 220 radar.

collision with a Bf 110 at Deelen in Holland. The first air combat success took place on the night of 18 June 1941, when Ofw Paul Gildner of 4./NJG 1 shot down two Wellingtons and a Whitley; Gildner would go on to claim ten RAF bombers flying the Do 215B-5. On 1 July 1941, command of 4./NJG 1 went to Oblt Helmut Lent and, the day after, he was given a familiarisation flight by Oblt Helmut Woltersdorf in the Do 215. Then, on his first flight with his new Staffel in the early hours of 4 July 1941, and flying the Do 215, Lent got his 13th victory: a 301 Sqn Wellington. However, his victory six days later on 10 July 1941 was hard fought and although the Wellington, flown by Plt Off Guy Conran of 40 Sqn, was shot down, Helmut's Do 215B-5 was hit by return fire. He received a graze on his left arm due to a splinter but his radio operator, Uffz Walter Kubisch, was hit in the head and his flight engineer, Fw Walter Matuschak, was also wounded. By 1 November 1941, Do 215s of 4./NJG 1 had claimed 20 RAF bombers and the only loss came on 26 October 1941 when an aileron on one came loose on an operational mission and the crew baled out over the sea, the only casualty being the pilot, Lt Karl Bock, who was killed. On 1 November 1941, Helmut Lent was given command of the newly formed II./NJG 2 with the Do 215s of 4./NJG 1 going to Oblt Egmont Prinz zur Lippe-Weissenfeld's 5 and Oblt Ludwig Becker's 6./NJG 2, the latter having already shot down six aircraft with the Do 215; it would go on to shoot down another 13. However, by January 1942, the Do 215 was being replaced, predominantly by the Bf 110. Although it soldiered on, in October 1942, the remaining eight Do 215B-5s with II./NJG 2 were transferred to IV./NJG 1, after which the survivors were transferred to Nachtjagdschule for training use. It is fitting that the last of 37 aircraft confirmed as having been shot down by Do 215s came on the night of 9 November 1942, when Maj Helmut Lent, now commanding IV./NJG 1, shot down a 102 Sqn Halifax for his 54th victory of the war.

Due to the rarity of the type, no complete examples of the Do 215 exist. However, on the night of 6 July 1941, Do 215B-5 Wk Nr 0046 G9+OM of 4./NJG 1, flown by Oblt Helmut Woltersdorf, ditched in the Waddenzee 2km east of Texel after being damaged by return fire from a 40 Sqn Wellington that they had just shot down. The crew escaped with varying degrees of injuries and the fighter settled onto the seabed in what would become a protected natural habitat; the remains were not recovered until 1992.

Do 217

The Do 217 bomber came into service in mid-1941 but with the Luftwaffe still needing more night-fighters, a Do 217E-2 was quickly modified by fitting four MG 17s and four MG FF 20mm cannon in a solid nose. The rear-firing guns, including the MG 131 in the turret, were retained, as was the ability to carry bombs to become the Do 217J-1, which was intended as a night intruder. However, even before it first flew, in October 1941, such missions over Britain ceased by order of the Führer. The J-1 was then fitted with the FuG 202 Lichtenstein BC airborne interception radar, and the J-2 with the FuG 212 Lichtenstein C-1.

Operational evaluation was carried out in March 1942 and, although it was found adequate, the Do 217J-1 was only delivered piecemeal to various operational and training units. It was not popular, as Oblt Wilhelm Herget of 4./NJG 1 wrote:

My Gruppe had a Staffel of Do 217s in 1943 because Bf 110s were in short supply and High Command thought that the four and half hour endurance compared to the two and a half of the Bf 110 could be of use. The 217 was fast, stable, excellent for instrument flying and obviously a very nice bomber but much too heavy on the controls for a fighter. I flew it once just to try it but after that I refused to use it on operations and stuck to my tried and tested 110 which was greatly superior as a fighter.

Do 217J-1 of 4./NJG 3, summer 1942.

Do 217N-0 fitted with the FuG 202.

Crews generally found the aircraft difficult to take off and land and that it had too little performance in reserve for a fighter, which was not helped by its poor manoeuvrability in combat. Furthermore, with both offensive and defensive armament, it was normal to carry 750kg of ammunition, which further affected the night-fighter's performance.

In July 1942, the Do 217N-1 first flew. It was identical to the J-2 but, like the Do 217M, was powered by DB 603 engines. It would later have the turret and rear-facing guns removed to become the N-2, which was fitted with obliquely mounted upward MG151 cannon in the fuselage – the so called Schräge Musik modification.

After 130 Do 217J-1s and J-2s and around 240 Do 217N-1s and N-2s (around 95 N-1s were converted to N-2s) had been built, in October 1943 production of the Do 217 ceased. All but a few operational units had handed over their Do 217s; some went to training units, some to Nachtaufklärungstaffel (Night Reconnaissance Squadron) and elements of NJG 4, and NJG 100 continued to operate a number over the Western and Eastern Fronts well into 1944. The Do 217Ns and Js equipped II./NJG 1, Stab, II and III./NJG 2, Ergänzungs/NJG 2, Stab, I, II, and IV./NJG 3, I, II and III./NJG 4, II and IV.//NJG 5 I., II and 7./NJG 100, 4./NJG 200 as well as the training units I. and II./NJG 101 and NJ Schule 1. However, numbers and duration with each unit varied.

The Italian Air Force did express an interest in the Do 217 as a night-fighter and, in August 1942, crews began training on it in Germany. A total of 12 were ordered (six J-1s and six J-2s) and were operated by 235a Squadriglia of 60° Gruppo 41° Stormo and 233a Squadrigila 59° Gruppo 41° Stormo Intercettori, both based at Lonate Pozzolo. 233a Squadriglia did not receive its first two Do 217s until 24 February 1943, when they became part of a mixed aircraft unit. However, after just five months, July 1943 would see the swan song of the Italian Do 217. 41° Stormo disbanded on 1 July, and 59° and 60° Gruppo (the former defending Turin, the latter Milan) became independent units. In all of its time operating over Italy, just one victory was recorded by an Italian Do 217 when, on the night of 16 July 1943, Capt Aramis Ammanato, the commander of 235a Squadriglia shot down a Lancaster south-west of Milan. By the end of July 1943, the Italians reported that, of the 11 aircraft, six were unserviceable and, due to a lack of spares, the last known sortie was flown on 16 August 1943, after which the unit began converting to the Reggiane 2001 single-seat fighter.

In January 1943, Hungary also expressed an interest in the Do 217 as a night-fighter but received three Bf 110s instead.

Above left: Do 217J clearly showing armament and radar aerials.

Above right: Do 217N-1.

Do 217N-2 of 6./NJG 4, which landed in Switzerland, 2 May 1944.

Do 217N-2 without radar aerials.

Chapter 7
Junkers Fighters

The aircraft manufacturer Junkers was better known for building bombers. However, two types – the Ju 88 and proposed Ju 388 – were also converted to, or built as, day or night fighters.

Ju 88

Originally designed as a three-person dive-bomber, the Ju 88 first became operational in September 1939. It then served throughout the war in all theatres in many different guises, including night-fighter, long-range intruder, tank-buster, train-buster, reconnaissance and torpedo aircraft, and was a prime example of the Luftwaffe's philosophy of taking a basic airframe and modifying or re-modifying it for numerous roles.

Junkers at its Dessau factory started work mid-January 1936 on two designs: a twin tailfin aircraft, known as the Ju 85, and a single-fin aircraft known as the Ju 88; it was the latter that was selected by the RLM in May 1936. Work began on three prototypes, the first of which was completed and flown on 21 December 1936. The Ju 88V1 was powered by two Daimler-Benz DB 600Aa engines as was the V2, which had modified radiator intakes. The V3, which first flew in September 1937, had Junkers Jumo 211A engines, a raised cabin roof, an additional rear-firing machine gun and an offset gondola that housed a bomb sight. This aircraft performed so well when evaluated that contracts were placed in early 1938. However, the RLM now wanted the Ju 88 to also be a dive-bomber with increased defensive armament. This resulted in the V4, which looked more like the later Ju 88s with its distinctive glazed

Above: Ju 88C-2 of Zerstörer Staffel/KG 30, Norway, May 1940.

Right: Ju 88C-4 of I./NJG 2, North Africa, 1942.

nose. The V5 then reverted to having no gondola, a solid nose cone and Jumo 211B engines as it was to be used for record-breaking flights, but it was the V6, which first flew in June 1938, that was the first production prototype. Subtle modifications followed with the fitment of dive brakes and bomb racks and after the V10, in March 1939, the Ju 88 A-1s began to leave the production line (albeit there were another five prototypes after the V10).

The first Ju 88 bombers were assigned to Erprobungskommando 88 in spring 1939 which, in August 1939, became I Gruppe/Kampfgeschwader 25 (I./KG 25) and soon after I./KG 30. I/.KG 30 flew its first operational flight over the North Sea on 26 September 1939. It lost its first Ju 88A-1 in action during an attack on British warships on 9 October 1939. However, performance deficiencies in the A-1 led to major redesign work. The outcome was the Ju 88A-4, which had improved engines, a longer (65ft 10 ½in) and improved wing span and a strengthened undercarriage. A-1s were now modified to A-4 specification and became the Ju 88A-5. Many units were equipped with this variant before the arrival of the bespoke A-4, production of which was hampered by a lack of Jumo 211J engines.

At the same time, Ju 88A-1s were having single 20mm MG FF cannon and three 7.92mm MG 17 machine guns fixed into a solid nose and these aircraft were renamed the Ju 88C-1 and C-2. It was clear that with its maximum speed of over 300mph (500kph), the Ju 88C-1 was comparable with the only other Zerstörer at that time, the Bf 110C. However, where the Ju 88C-1 was superior was its range of over 1,400 miles (2,250km) with internal fuel, compared to the Bf 110's range of over 560 miles (around 900km). To increase its range, the Bf 110 required either a non-jettisonable ventral tank or two underwing tanks, all of which had a detrimental effect on its combat performance.

In February 1940, the first, and as it would transpire only, batch of 20 Ju 88C-1s (sometimes known as Ju 88Zs) were available. To operationally test these aircraft, a new unit was formed on 21 February 1940. The only fully operational Ju 88 unit at that time was KG 30, so it was decided to form Zerstörer Staffel./KG 30 (Z.St./KG 30) which was subordinate to both I./KG 30 and the Ju 88 training unit, Ergänzungsgruppe 4 (formerly Lehrgruppe Ju 88). Command of the Staffel went to Oblt Herbert Bönsch, while crews were posted in mainly from Bf 110 units. Initially, the Staffel was expected to have 13 crews and 15 aircraft but the first Ju 88s did not arrive until around the middle of March 1940 and by 9 April 1940 (the start of the German invasion of Norway), it had 12 crews and just six aircraft based at Perleberg, but Z.St./KG 30 had not yet been declared fully combat ready. Nevertheless, the first air combat victories went to Ofw Martin Jeschke and Uffz Peters Lauffs over Norway on 12 April 1940.

At the end of the Norway campaign, Z.St./KG 30 returned to Germany and, in July 1940, was re-designated II./Nachtjagdgeschwader 1 (II./NJG 1), a night-fighter unit. In September 1940, this then became I./NJG 2 and this Gruppe, which also operated a few Do 17Z-7s and Z-10s, was active in the intruder role over England until October 1941, attacking RAF airfields both with gunfire and dropping up to eight SC50 bombs, after which it went to operate over Malta. The Ju 88C-2 would evolve into the Ju 88C-4 (different engines, the bomb equipment removed and new propellers) and, ultimately, the Ju 88C-6, which was purpose-built as a night-fighter but would also be used in daylight as a heavy fighter in Russia (on train-busting missions), the Mediterranean (as a convoy escort) and, more notably, over the Bay of Biscay with the unit V./KG 40 (which, in October 1943, became I./Zerstörergeschwader 1). From mid-1942, the V./KG 40 unit was used for U-boat, shipping and aircraft escort, armed reconnaissance and, more often than not, in the pure fighter role against Allied aircraft.

There would then be two variants of the Ju 88 night-fighter, which would replace the Ju 88C-6. The Ju 88R was both a night-fighter and a day heavy fighter, which was essentially a Ju 88C-6 fitted with BMW 801A engines and would be designated the Ju 88R-1. It was designed to have more power and speed than the C-6 but the armament remained unchanged. The RAF managed to obtain a pristine example of a Ju 88R-1 when, on 9 May 1943, a crew from 10./NJG 3 defected and landed in Scotland.

In addition to being used as a night-fighter, it too was operated in daylight, especially by V./KG 40 and then I./ZG 1 over the Bay of Biscay, Mediterranean and, for the first week in June 1944, as a daylight ground-attack aircraft over Normandy (where the unit was decimated by Allied aircraft and flak, which led to the unit's disbandment). I. and later III./ZG 1 used the R-2 variant, losing its first aircraft in an accident on 29 January 1944. The R-2 differed to the R-1 by being powered by BMW 801D engines, as opposed to the BMW 801A, which necessitated modifications to the engine cowlings. The armament was unchanged but the R-2 had increased armour, in particular an armoured windscreen. The ultimate Ju 88 night-fighter was the purpose-designed Ju 88G. This version was intended to be cleaner in looks, faster and more heavily armed utilising the Ju 188 fuselage and tailplane. The Ju 88G-1 was powered by two BMW 801G engines and therefore looked similar to the Ju 88R-1 apart from the improved more angular tail. In addition to increased protective armour, it was armed with six belt-fed 20mm MG151 cannon – two in the nose and four in an offset belly pack – and an MG 131 for rearwards defensive fire, and it could also be fitted with the Schräge Musik obliquely mounted 20mm cannon as well as being able to carry bombs. The RAF also managed to obtain a pristine example of a Ju 88G-1 when, on 13 July 1944, an aircraft from 7./NJG 2 landed in error at RAF Woodbridge in Suffolk.

The Ju 88G-1 began leaving the production line in late 1943 and would be followed mid-1944 by the Ju 88G-6, which was powered by Jumo 213E engines. This would be followed by the final production model, the Ju 88G-7, which was powered by Jumo 213E-1 engines and had extended wings (from the Ju 188). However, the first Ju 88 G-7 was not allocated to a unit until the end of March 1945 – too late to make any significant impact on the night air war. All the Ju 88 night-fighters were equipped with airborne radar, namely FuG 202, 212 or 220 Lichtenstein, FuG 227 Flensburg, FuG 350 Naxos, FuG 218 Neptun and FuG 240 Berlin.

Over 15,000 Ju 88s were produced and, as a result, quite a number (or their remains) exist in museums and private collections around the world. The most impressive example of a night-fighter can be found in the RAF Museum London, which has the Ju 88R-1 Wk Nr 360043 coded D5+EV of 10/NJG 3, which was flown by its crew to RAF Dyce in Scotland on 9 May 1943.

Above left: Ju 88C-6 of V./KG 40 clearly showing its armament.

Above right: Ju 88C-6s of V./KG 40, France, 1943.

Ju 388J

The Ju 188 was essentially a bomber and reconnaissance replacement for the Ju 88. Despite the war turning against Germany, other variants of the Ju 188 were planned, including the Ju 188J, a heavy fighter or night-fighter, and the Ju 188R night-fighter. However, production was switched to the Ju 388 and this did not progress further.

Named by Adolf Hitler in March 1945 as the Störtebeker, after the legendary German privateer Klaus Störtebeker, the Ju 388J, together with the Ju 388L (reconnaissance) and the Ju 388K (bomber), was a further development of the Ju 188; it was a fighter with a pressurised cockpit so that it could carry out high-altitude interceptions in response to the fear that the Americans would start operating the B-29 Superfortress over Germany.

In September 1943, the Hubertus Programme called for the design, development and manufacture of up to 400 Ju 388s a month at seven different locations. The basic armament for all three variants was intended to be a single remote turret in the tail, armed with two MG 131 13mm guns, which would be operated via a periscope located in the cockpit. The Ju 388J would also have either two 30mm and two 20mm cannon in a hardened nose, as opposed to a Perspex nose and an obliquely mounted 30mm Schräge Musik cannon behind the cockpit. The engines would either be BMW 801Js, Jumo 222 A/Bs or Jumo 213 Es, but the Jumo 222 failed to make it past testing and was never used.

The Ju 388V1 prototype first flew in December 1943, after which another seven prototypes followed, the trials being successfully completed by mid-March 1944. As a night-fighter equipped with FuG 218 Neptun radar, in trials, the Ju 388J-1 had the potential to be a first-class night and all-weather fighter and the decision was made to not fit it with the remote turret. However, engine shortages, and then further delays in supplying them, added to the unlikely appearance of the B-29 over Germany, which was now being sent to the Pacific; only three Ju 388J prototypes are thought to have been produced from an order of 594 to be built by Allgemeine Transportanlagen-Gesellschaft at a rate of 40 per month. These were delivered in September 1944 and, shortly after, production of the J and K ceased, with the Ju 388L now being the main priority. Just 105 Ju 388s were built in total, excluding the prototypes, of which just 23 were delivered to the Luftwaffe. It is possible that NJG 2 operated a number of pre-production Ju 388Js for operational evaluation in the last few weeks of the war but this cannot be positively confirmed. Japan, similarly mindful of the B-29 threat, apparently expressed an interest in manufacturing the Ju 388 under licence, but nothing transpired so late in the war. At least three examples were captured intact: the Soviets captured one, the RAF captured a Ju 188L-1, Wk Nr 500006 (formerly Ju 388V6), and the Americans a Ju 388L-1, Wk Nr 560049, but no fighter variants were captured. The RAF example was scrapped but the American example is still in existence at the Paul E Garber Preservation, Restoration, and Storage Facility, part of the National Air and Space Museum, Suitland, Maryland.

Above left and above right: Ju 88R-1 of 10./NJG 3, whose crew defected to Scotland on 9 May 1943.

Above: Ju 88C-6 of 14./KG 40, France, 1943.

Right: Ju 88R-2 of 1./ZG 1, France, 1944.

Below left: Ju 88G-6 captured at the end of the war, showing SN2 radar aerials.

Below right: Captured Ju 88G-6 fitted with the FuG 218 Neptun radar.

Above left: Ju 88G-6 of Stab./NJG 5 captured in Denmark at the end of the war. The first photo shows FuG 220 and Naxos aerials; the second photo shows the Schrage Musik guns.

Above right: Ju 88 G-7 fitted with the FuG 240 Berlin radar.

Left: Ju 88C-6 of Stab I./NJG 2 captured at Schelswig at the end of the war.

Below: Ju 388J-1 Störtebeker.

Chapter 8
Zerstörers Over the Med

On 4 September 1942, the Allies confirmed I./NJG 2 had departed from the Mediterranean for Belgium and left 26 Ju 88Cs behind, seven of which would be assigned to 10./ZG 26 at Derna. 10./ZG 26 had been formed in March 1942 with eight Do 17s and was based in Crete; its task was to escort convoys between Greece and Crete, predominantly in daylight. The replacement of the Do 17s with Ju 88C-6s began in September 1942 and two months later all the Do 17s had gone.

New Zerstörers

10./ZG 26 was commanded by Oblt Peter Habicht. He was an experienced pre-war civilian flying instructor. He had first joined 7./ZG 26 in 1941, flying Bf 110s, and was injured in an accident on 8 November 1941. He claimed his first victory, an unidentified 'Boeing' off Malta on 22 February 1942, while with 8./ZG 26, and took command of 10./ZG 26 on 27 August 1942.

The first recorded loss for a Ju 88C-4 of 10./ZG 26 occurred at Derna on 7 September 1942 when one crash-landed for non-combat reasons, killing Uffz Gerhard Franze and two crew members. The first combat loss occurred on 12 October 1942, when the Ju 88C-6, flown by Fw Hugo Brückner, force-landed at Ayn al-Ġazāla following combat; the pilot and one crew member were wounded. No Allied claims can match with this but, on 19 November 1942, two aircraft were involved in combat with what was believed to be Kittyhawks of 250 Sqn 10 miles off Martuba. Fg Off Gordon Troke and Fg Off James Collier claimed a Ju 88 destroyed and possibly one damaged. 10./ZG 26 reported one being shot down east of Appolonia, while a second aircraft returned to Sidi el Magrun but crashed on landing. Lt Theodor Schuster and his crew were reported missing from the former aircraft, while the latter, again flown by the unlucky Fw Hugo Brückner, saw two of its crew being killed, while it appears Bruckner remained uninjured.

The first air combat claim for the Staffel was filed on 25 October 1942. Two Ju 88C-6s of 10./ZG 26, which were about to take up escort of a convoy named Alfredo, off Tobruk, reported being attacked by two Beaufighters, and Oblt Peter Habicht claimed to have shot one of them down. There was quite a battle over this convoy, with Beaufighters of 252 Sqn claiming to have shot down a Do 24 (which was

Above left: Ju 88C-6 of 4./NJG 1, autumn 1941.

Above right: Ju 88C-6 of 2./NJG 2, Benghasi, summer, 1942. Shortly afterwards, I./NJG 2 returned to Belgium, leaving its aircraft with 10./ZG 26.

The main opponent of 10. and 11./ZG 26: Beaufighters of 252 Sqn, see here on patrol over the Mediterranean.

in fact an Italian Cant Z.501), and escorting Ju 88 of 3./LG 1 into the sea and badly damaging another of 12./LG 1, which crash-landed at Cyrenaika. Bf 110s of 9./ZG 26 claimed to have shot down four Beaufighters 45 minutes later, but it appears that dates were getting confused by the Germans as the only Beaufighter to be lost on 25 October 1942 was flown by Wg Cdr John White of 272 Sqn, which is believed to have collided with a Ju 52. Habicht's claim would be the first and only claim for 10./ZG 26.

For the next five months, 10./ZG 26 appears to have carried out its business without incident – no claims or losses. By means of example, Fw Hermann Bolten had been involved with tactical trials of the Me 210 with the Erprobungsstaffel 210 from July 1942 and, at the end of October 1942, he flew to the

Above left and above right: Photographs of 10 and 11./ZG 26 are rare, but these show Ju 88C-6s during their time in the Mediterranean.

Mediterranean for further operational trials. His unit was now designated 16./KG 6 and was subordinate to 10./ZG 26 and he flew his first mission, a convoy escort from Kastelli, on 4 November 1942. After 18 operational flights over the Mediterranean in the Me 210, he then flew a Ju 88C-6 from Chinisia on 18 January 1943 with 10./ZG 26. He would fly 19 operational flights in the Ju 88, all of them daylight ship or convoy escorts, before moving back to Germany after 6 February 1943 to join the Erprobungsstaffel Me 410 at Lechfeld.

By April 1943, 10./ZG 26 had an establishment of up to 18 aircraft, but only half were available at any one time. The first combat loss of the year came on 20 April 1943 when a Ju 88C-6 was reported shot down 50km west of the island of Marettimo, west of Sicily, after combat with 'P-51s', killing Uffz Hans Köhler and his crew. It is probable they were shot down north-west of Cape Bon between 0555–0735hrs by 2d Lt John P Bedford and Capt Fred A Borsodi Bon of 86th Fighter Sqn/79th Fighter Gp. However, there were other claims for Ju88s by 112 Sqn and 2 Sqn South African Air Force (SAAF) five miles off Ras el Mar, the successful South African pilots being Capt L C H Hope and Lt G Oglivie Watson. All three units flew P-40s/Kittyhawks. A second Ju 88C-6 was damaged on its return to Trapani from an operational mission on 20 April 1943.

10./ZG 26 would then suffer three accidents before the end of June 1943, which resulted in the deaths of pilots Fw Franz Behringer (6 June), Fw Wilhelm Heining (10 June) and Ofw Kurt Bonnemann (26 June). Then, on 25 August 1943, aircraft flown by Uffz Otto Müller and Lt Wilhelm Debes collided east of the island of Euboea, east of Athens, killing both crews. The following month, 10./ZG 26 was withdrawn to Germany and in November 1943 it became 7./ZG 76, based at Öttingen and re-equipped with Bf 110s. As to its Staffelkapitän, Peter Habicht would be awarded the Ehrenpokal on 30 April 1943 and on 17 October 1943 he was awarded the Deutsches Kreuz in Gold. He appears to have then been posted to command the Ergänzungs Zerstörer Gruppe in mid-September 1943 but would be shot down and killed on 11 January 1944 near Ottleben, near Magdeburg, flying an Me 410A-1.

Reformation

Notwithstanding the transfer of 10./ZG 26 back to Germany, on 16 May 1943, 11./ZG 26 was formed at Athens-Kalamaki using half of 10./ZG 26's aircraft, to which new aircraft were moved in, taking its establishment to a maximum of 11 aircraft. Its primary task was still convoy escort between Greece and Crete and, more generally, in the Aegean. Later, and as the war turned more against Germany, a secondary task was considered to have been anti-partisan missions in Yugoslavia and Greece, but little evidence of this has surfaced. It is possible that Oblt Peter Habicht initially commanded the Staffel before command went to Hptm Wilhelm Pflanz, another long-serving Bf 110 pilot with ZG 26. Again, very little is known about Pflanz and this unit.

11./ZG 26 moved to Athens-Eleusis in June 1943, suffering its first casualties on 27 June 1943 when two Ju 88C-6s were damaged during the bombing of the airfield. It appears it was then involved in operations off Kos, Leros and Samos from September 1943 onwards and lost its first aircraft and crew on 18 September 1943, when Ofw Heinz Gründling went missing off Rhodes. Then, on 12 November 1943, Lt Hans Sukowski and Uffz Gregor Merva and their crews failed to return from operations off Leros. There were no Allied claims that could match with these three losses, although four 47 Sqn Beaufighters and three B-25s of 310st Bomb Group, escorted by six Beaufighters of 603 Sqn, did attack a convoy off Leros during the afternoon of 12 November 1943. Despite reporting seeing German aircraft, no mention was made of any combats with Ju 88s, even if a Beaufighter from 47 Sqn was lost. Hans Sukowski had only joined 11./ZG 26 on 23 October 1943. His first operational flight had been a fighter sweep between Athens and Rhodes on the afternoon of 30 October 1943 where he reported combat with two Beaufighters, probably those flown by WO Harry Nice and Sgt Eilwyn James of 227 Sqn, south of the island of Kastellorizo. Sukowski's death occurred on his fourth operational flight.

Ju 88C-6s protecting a warship, Mediterranean, 1943.

There were then two claims made by two unidentified NCO pilots from 11./ZG 26 on 16 November 1943 (the day that British troops surrendered on Leros) for two Beaufighters over the Aegean. That day, 47 Sqn and 603 Sqn attacked a Siebel ferry off Kalymnos, which was carrying troops to reinforce Leros. As well as a surface escort, the ferry was also accompanied by seven Ar 196s, four Bf 109s and four Ju 88s. Despite hitting the ferry, which then caught fire and sank, Beaufighters flown by Fg Offs Bill Thwaites, Tony Bond and John Fletcher were shot down. However, at the same time as the 11./ZG 26 claims, Bf 109s of III./JG 27, led by Maj Ernst Düllberg, claimed three Beaufighters in the Levita/Kos/Tría Nisiá area.

1944 would see 11./ZG 26 continuing with escort duties. In January 1944, the unit reported just eight aircraft available, a number that would rise to a maximum of 26 by May 1944, but just three aircraft would be lost in the first six months of 1944. The first came on 31 January 1944. Eight Beaufighters of 252 Sqn, led by Flt Lt Reg Meyer, took off on an offensive shipping search in the eastern Aegean. When off the northern tip of Stampalia, they intercepted three Ju 88s; Meyer was credited with shooting one down but, at the same time, a Beaufighter flown by Fg Off Darrell Hall was seen to have crashed into the sea close to where the Ju 88 had crashed. The Ju 88C-6 was from 11./ZG 26 and flown by Uffz Franz Grüber, whose Bordfunker, Uffz Friedrich Stoll, was credited with shooting down a Beaufighter before the German crew were shot down and killed. One of the other German pilots involved, Uffz Herbert Glöge, reported getting into combat with 'four Mitchells' and that one was shot down for the loss of one Ju 88. RAF crews that day reported a Bf 109 seen during the combat, while another Beaufighter, flown by Flt Sgt F A Stevenson, force-landed in Turkey.

It now appears to have been quiet for 11./ZG 26 until the start of June 1944 when, on 8 June, a Ju 88C-6 flown by Ofw Heinrich Schiller crashed 10km east of Cape Santa Maria di Leuca and, on 9 June, Uffz Günter König was reported missing on operations. Flt Lt Don Pinks and his navigator/radiographer Flt Sgt Maurice Noble of 255 Sqn, while on an anti-reconnaissance patrol, reported shooting down a Ju 88 off 'Cap Maria de Leuca' at 0427hrs on 9 June 1944, which was possibly that flown by König.

Disbandment and disappearance

These would be the last operational losses for 11./ZG 26 as, at the start of September 1944, the Staffel was recalled from the Mediterranean. Hptm Wilhelm Pflanz was awarded the Ehrenpokal on 8 May 1944 but shortly after is believed to have handed command over to Hptm Richard Riedel. One more loss would still occur when, on 2 September 1944, a Ju 88C-6 crashed near Mauthausen in Austria on its way northwards, killing Uffz Walter Baumann, two crew members, an engineer and a passenger. By 10 September 1944, 23 Ju 88C-6s of 11./ZG 26 were reported being with Luftflotte 5 at Oerlandet in Denmark, a number which had reduced to 16 by 20 November 1944, but few if any operational flights were carried out and, in November 1944, 11./ZG 26 began converting to the Me 410 in preference over the Ju 88C-6. The Ju88C-6s languished there until the end of February 1945 when 16 of them were assigned to the reconnaissance unit 1 Staffel(Fern)/Aufklärungsgruppe 120 but whether they were ever used in this new role is not known.

It has been suggested that in addition to daylight escort missions, 10. And 11./ZG 26 carried out night-fighter missions. However, of those few logbooks which have surfaced since 1945, this cannot be substantiated.

Chapter 9
Life and Death of an Ace

Few German fighter pilots fought throughout World War Two, and even fewer also flew with the Condor Legion in Spain. Günther Lützow was one pilot who did, and who sadly lost his life exactly two weeks before the war ended.

Early years

Günther 'Franzl' Lützow was born in Kiel on 4 September 1912, the son of Admiral Friedrich and Hildegard Lützow, and the third of five children. His father had joined the Imperial Navy as a cadet in 1899 and, during World War Two, served with distinction on both warships, including commanding the small cruiser *Hamburg* and submarines and, at the end of the war, commanding the U-boat flotilla at Pola. However, 'Franzl' did not follow his father into the navy; he joined the army in 1930 and began flying training the following year at the Deutsche Verkehrsfliegerschule at Schleissheim. His brothers did join the Kriegsmarine, Werner being killed in action commanding 4 Schnellbootflottille on 24 November 1943, while Joachim survived the war having commanded a minesweeper. Still serving as an infantry junior officer, Günther then undertook fighter pilot training at the secret facility at Lipetsk in Russia. In 1934, he transferred to the Luftwaffe, joining the Reklamestafffel in Döberitz (a cover name for Jagdgeschwader 132 [JG 132]) as an instructor, still holding the rank of Leutnant, after which he became an instructor at the Jagdfliegerschule (JFS) at Schleissheim. In 1936, he became the adjutant of JG 132 with the rank of Oberleutnant and later that year it is believed he took command of 4./JG 132.

Into combat

Lützow arrived in Spain and took command of the Bf 109-equipped 2.J/88 from Hptm Siegfried Lehmann on 19 March 1937. He would go on to shoot down five aircraft in Spain, his first being a Curtiss on 6 April 1937, his last a Rata on 22 August 1937. On 6 September 1937 he handed over to Hptm Joachim Schlichting and would be promoted to Hptm himself shortly after his return. He took command of 5./JG 132 only to be posted to command 3./JFS 1 at Werneuchen in November 1937, where

Below left: Günther Lützow (left) escorting Obstlt Theo Osterkamp. This photo was taken at JFS 1, Werneuchen, which Osterkamp commanded from April 1937 to the outbreak of war, while Lützow commanded 3./JFS 1 from November 1937.

Below right: Bf 109E-1s of J/88 in Spain.

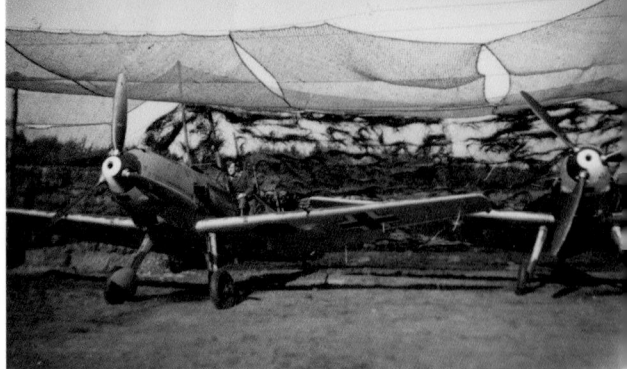

Above left: Lützow with Oblt Johannes Loidolt of 3./JG 3. Loidolt was shot down and taken prisoner on 31 August 1940 after his Bf 109 E-4 crashed at Chadwell Heath, Essex.

Above right: Bf 109E-4s of I./JG 3, spring–summer 1940. It is possible the aircraft on the left was Lützow's.

his experiences as a fighter pilot in Spain were passed on to trainee fighter pilots. It was there in early 1938 that he met his future wife, Gisela von Preisdorf, and they were married in Berlin in March 1939. In November 1939, he took command of I./JG 3 at Zerbst from Obstlt Otto-Heinrich von Houwald and after a quiet Phoney War (his Gruppe recorded neither victories nor combat losses) he was still leading the I./JG 3 at the start of the Battle of France. During this time, his son, Hans-Ulrich, was born; a daughter, Carola, would be born in August 1942.

Operating from Hargimont, his first and second victories of World War Two came on 14 May 1940 when he claimed two Curtiss fighters north-west of Dinant. I./JG 3 claimed a total of eight French fighters that evening and it is believed their victims were Bloch 152s from Groupe de Chasse (GC) 6/10 (which lost one aircraft) and GC III/10 (which lost another six). It has been suggested that Lützow's victims were Lt Pierre Martin, who baled out wounded near Ragnies, and Adjutant Marcel Schneider, who force-landed near Le Hérie-la-Vieville. He would claim another Curtiss the following day and by 3 June 1940, he had shot down a total of seven French aircraft. On 3 June 1940, he shot down his first RAF aircraft, believed to have been a Blenheim of 40 Sqn flown by Sqn Ldr Brian Paddon. The Blenheim crashed between St Valéry and Abbeville. Although two of the crew were captured, Paddon managed to evade the enemy initially but was later captured, after which he became a serial escaper, returning to Britain after his 11th attempt in August 1942. Two days later, Günther claimed his second RAF aircraft, a Blenheim believed to be from 21 Sqn flown by Fg Off Hugh Dunford-Wood who, with his other two crew members, was killed. This would be Lützow's ninth and final victory of the Battle of France.

Battle of Britain

By the start of the Battle of Britain, I./JG 3 was located at Grandvilliers south-south-west of Poix in northern France, moving to Colembert east-north-east of Boulogne on 1 August 1940. Lützow would claim just one victory with I./JG 3 in the Battle of Britain, a Spitfire on the evening of 16 August 1940. On 21 August 1940, he took command of the Geschwader from Obstlt Carl Vieck, with command of I./JG 3 going to Hptm Hans von Hahn, formerly of 8./JG 53, six days later. His first victory as Kommodore was on 26 August 1940 when he and his adjutant, Oblt Friedrich-Franz von Cramon, claimed three Boulton Paul Defiants while escorting Do 17s of Kampfgeschwader 3 attacking RAF Manston. 264 Sqn reported three Defiants shot down in the area of Herne Bay – Sgt Edward Thorne crash-landed east of Margate, while Flt Lt Arthur Banham and Fg Off Ian Stephenson were shot down into Herne Bay. Arthur Banham wrote afterwards:

> When approaching Dover at 12,000ft, we sighted 12 Do 17s in vics line astern. We approached on starboard side in two vics line astern and I opened fire at leading bomber of last section. I saw my gunner get in a long burst at 100yds; I then broke away and turned towards leading section and got a long burst

in at 100yds on No. 2 of first section. I was then hit myself near the cockpit and my machine was on fire. I lost control and telling my gunner to jump as I turned aircraft on its back. I fell out and was picked up in the sea.

By the time he was awarded the Ritterkreuz on 18 September 1940, Lützow's score stood at 15, and by the end of 1940, it had risen to 18. He would score no more victories on the Channel Front in 1941, but on 7 May 1941, his Bf 109F-2 was slightly damaged in combat. It is believed the combat took place mid-morning between Calais and Dover, as Hptm Gordon Gollob Staffelkapitän of 4./JG 3 was the only victim from the Geschwader that day at the hands of a Spitfire off Gravelines at 1125hrs, flown by either Sgt Harold Hall of 54 Sqn or Sgt Jack Claxton of 611 Sqn. A number of pilots from 74 and 611 Sqns claimed to have damaged Bf 109s, so it is not possible to identify who might have damaged Lutzow's fighter.

JG 3 would now remain in France for one month and one day more as they moved east to Breslau and then to Hostynne-Zamosc in Poland, which is where they were when Germany attacked the Soviet Union on 22 June 1941.

Barbarossa

Lützow's first kill in the East (his 19th) came on the first day of the attack when he shot down his 40th aircraft on 17 July 1941; he was awarded the Eichenlaub (Oakleaves) to the Ritterkreuz three days later. On 17 September 1941, his Bf 109F was apparently damaged by flak and he force-landed behind Soviet lines but quickly returned. On 11 October 1941, he was awarded the Schwerter (Swords) to the Ritterkreuz, with his score standing at 92. His 100th and 101st kills came on 24 October 1941, and he was promoted to Obstlt a few days after this. Following these victories, it would appear that, due to being the second German fighter pilot to claim 100 aircraft in combat, he was restricted in the number of operational flights he would now fly. By this stage, he was commanding JG 51 as well as JG 3 following Maj Friedrich Beckh being wounded on 16 September 1941. However, JG 3 was moved back to Germany in early November 1941, and shortly after arriving at Wiesbaden-Erbenheim, Generaloberst Ernst Udet, a former World War One ace and the Luftwaffe's Director General of Equipment, committed suicide on 17 November 1941; Lützow was part of the honour guard for his funeral. The following month, JG 3 was

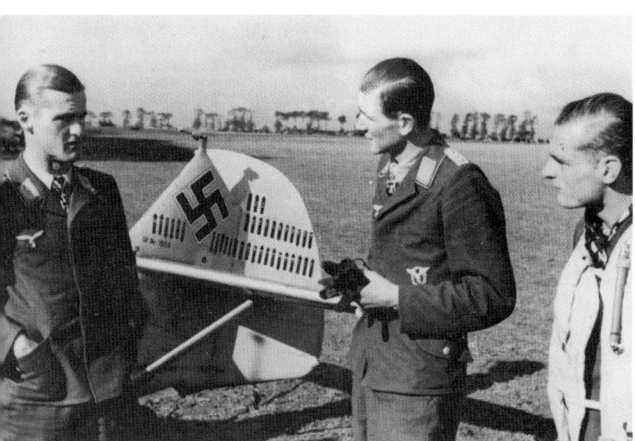

Above left: Lützow, Hptm Wilhelm Balthasar and Oblt Egon Troha (Staffelkapitän of 9./JG 3). The rudder of Balthasar's Bf 109E-4 Wk Nr 559 can be seen in the backgorund. Troha would be shot down and taken prisoner on 29 October 1940.

Above right: Lützow's Bf 109E-4 Wk Nr 3742 seen at Desvres during the Battle of Britain.

given the honorary title 'Udet' in the Generaloberst's memory. JG 3 did not return to the Eastern Front until mid-May 1942 and Lützow scored his 102nd victory on 21 May 1942. Two days later, his Bf 109F-4 suffered a technical problem and he force-landed at Tschuhgujew, but he was apparently uninjured. On 11 August 1942, he handed over the Geschwader to Hptm Wolf-Dietrich Wilcke, his last success with JG 3 being his 103rd victory on 29 July 1942. It would be another two and a half years before he would fly again on operations, and even then it would be short-lived.

Staff officer

Lützow then became Inspekteur der Tagjagd (Inspector of Day Fighters) for the Eastern Front, working for General Adolf Galland. In April 1943, he was promoted to Oberst and became Inspekteur der Tagjagd of the Italian Front in July 1943. Two months later, he took command of 1 Jagddivision, which was responsible for

Lützow with his wife and son, 1941.

the defence of north-west Germany. However, he fell foul of his immediate superior, Generalmajor Beppo Schmidt, and was relieved of his command in March 1944, being replaced by Oberst Hajo Hermann, a former bomber and single-seat night-fighter pilot who, himself, would later be relieved of his command for similar reasons. Lützow was posted to command 4 Fliegerschuldivision, responsible for training fighter pilots.

At the end of January 1945, after what became known as the Fighter Pilots' Mutiny, he was relieved of his post, as were Adolf Galland and a number of other successful senior and highly decorated fighter pilots, for openly criticising the Luftwaffe's senior commanders, in particular Reichsmarschall Hermann Göring, and was apparently posted to be Jafü Oberitalien and banned from returning to Germany. With the tide of war very much turned against Germany, at the start of April 1944 he joined Adolf Galland's Me 262-equipped JV 44 as its operations officer and at last returned to operational flying. He would not live to see the end of the war.

Final combat

During his short time with JV 44, Lützow would be credited with shooting down two American bombers. The date of the first is not certain but in the afternoon of 24 April 1945 he was one of six Me 262s scrambled from Riem to intercept B-26 Marauders of the 17th Bomb Group, which were attacking ammunition dumps at Schwabmünchen in southern Germany. Led by Lützow, two aborted with technical problems, leaving Hptm Walter Krupinski, Lt Klaus Neumann, an unidentified pilot and Lützow to intercept.

Both Krupinski and Neumann were Ritterkreuz holders and very successful fighter pilots in their own right. At least two of the Me 262s were equipped with R4M rockets, and it is believed that Lützow and Neumann each shot down a B-26; the 34th Bomb Squadron reporting the loss of aircraft flown by Lt Fred Harms and Lt Leigh Slates, the former crashing at Oberroth, the latter at Unterschönegg. However, P-47 Thunderbolts flown by Capt Jerry Mast and Lt William Myers of 388th Fighter Squadron/365 Fighter Group reported chasing an Me 262, which crashed near Schrobenhausen at 1525hrs. The following report was submitted by William Myers:

> I was flying Red Two position on Maj J R Hill's wing on an escort mission. Near the target area, four Me 262s bounced the bombers. During the ensuing dog fight, I saw a single Me 262 heading towards Red Flt. At this time I started to call Elwood Red Leader as to the position of the plane but he banked sharply and I thought he had already seen him. A minute later I heard someone call "I lost him." Believing this was my leader, I immediately rolled over and dove down on the aircraft which was now heading down. I headed straight down cutting him off indicating better than 600mph. I figured I could shoot him down as soon as he started to pull out. He started to pull out once but apparently saw either Capt Mast's or my own plane bearing down on him and immediately went into a steeper dive from which he never recovered. He hit the ground and exploded. I had to black myself out to keep from hitting the ground.

The only recorded loss that day was the Me 262 flown by Lützow, who was last seen near Donauwörth, about 50km north-west of Schrobenhausen. Walter Krupinski reported seeing an explosion on the ground, which afterwards was assumed to have been the crash of Lützow's Me 262.

After the war, surviving pilots came to the conclusion that Lützow was not comfortable in the Me 262 and, despite being an experienced and successful fighter pilot until the summer of 1942, he had lost his edge, and possibly his nerve, and his demise was inevitable. No wreckage has ever been found and Günther 'Franzl' Lützow is still reported as missing.

Above left: Lützow greeting Adolf Hitler, who was visiting JG 3 in December 1940. (via Oliver)

Above right: Lützow and fellow pilots hunting, winter 1940. (via Oliver)

Right: Lützow in the early stages of Operation *Barbarossa*, June–July 1941. (via Oliver)

Above left: Oberst Günther Lützow wearing the Ritterkreuz mit Schwertern, which he was awarded in October 1941.

Above right: Obstlt Werner Mölders (centre) handed over JG 51 to Maj Friedrich Beckh on 19 July 1941, but Beckh was wounded on 16 September 1941 and Lützow (right) took temporary command of JG 51 in addition to JG 3. To the left is Hptm Karl-Gottfried Nordmann, who took command of IV./JG 51 from Beckh and would be awarded the Ritterkreuz in August 1941.

Left: Galland (left) and Lützow (right) heading the honour guard for Ernst Udet's funeral, 22 November 1941.

Below: A pair of Me 262s scrambling to intercept Allied aircraft, 1944.

R4M rockets fitted to an Me 262A.

Me 262 A-1a of Kommando Nowotny, November 1944.

Chapter 10

One Man's *Barbarossa*: The Invasion of The Soviet Union as Experienced by a German Fighter Pilot

For those Luftwaffe fighter pilots who had experienced the Battle of France and the Battle of Britain, the invasion of the Soviet Union would be a totally different experience, as Hans Ohly found out.

Hans was born in 1915 and joined the German Navy in April 1934. Following basic training, he commenced flying training in November 1936 (having by then transferred to the Luftwaffe). A year later, having been promoted to Leutnant, he joined I Gruppe/Jagdgeschwader 134 (I./JG 134) in Dortmund, flying the Arado 65 and Arado 68. In the middle of 1938, I/JG 134 converted to the Messerschmitt 109D but then Ohly was posted to I./JG 131 at Jesau in East Prussia, where he flew a mix of single-engined fighters before being posted to Zerstörergeschwader 142 back in Dortmund. He spent just under two months with this unit before being posted to Jagdfliegerschule 2 at Schleissheim, where he would remain from March to December 1939. Oblt Ohly then joined the Messerschmitt Bf 109E-equipped 1./JG 53 at

Above left: Oblt Hans Ohly.

Above right: Ohly sitting in his Bf 109F-2, France, April 1941.

Above left: Ohly with his mechanic, April 1941.

Above right: Pilots of 1./JG 53 shortly before departing for Russia. Back left: Lt Walter Zellot, Uffz Wolfgang Bubenzer († 22 May 1941), Lt Ernst-Albrecht Schulz, Oblt Hans Ohly, Lt Wolfgang Hauffe, Lt Udo Padior. Front left: Gefr Heinz Sieg (wounded 29 May 1941), Fw Heinrich Rühl († 4 Jun 1941), Ofw Norbert Schäfer, Uffz Ludwig Reibel.

Darmstadt and would remain with 1./JG 53, originally commanded by experienced fighter pilot Hptm Werner Mölders but now by Ohly's friend, Oblt Hans-Karl Mayer, for the next 20 months.

Into action

Ohly's first operational flight took place on 30 December 1939 but his second, three days later, was almost his last. Taking off at 1347hrs on a flight over the front line, he was attacked by Curtiss H-75s of Group de Chasse II/5. 1./JG 53 came off worse in the combat, with Lt Walter Rupp landing his damaged fighter at Wiesbaden-Erbenheim while Hans, who had been slightly wounded in combat possibly with Lt Robert Huvet, force-landed his fighter near St Wendel. His wounds meant he did not return to flying duties until 7 May 1940, three days before the start of the Battle of France.

Ohly's first success came on 14 May 1940 when he shot down two RAF Bristol Blenheims and a Fairey Battle. However, by the end of the Battle of France, he had flown nearly 50 operational sorties but had not increased his score. His first kill of the Battle of Britain would come on 25 August 1940 (a Hurricane near Portland) and a few days later his Geschwader moved to Pas-de-Calais. He was then given command of 1./JG 53 while Hans-Karl Mayer was given command of I./JG 53 in the afternoon of 2 September (and awarded the Ritterkreuz the following day). Mayer would be killed in action on 17 October 1940.

Ohly's last Battle of Britain mission was in the afternoon of 28 October 1940 – an escort for the fighter-bombers of 3./JG 53. 1./JG 53 would remain at Étaples in France until 20 December 1940 when it withdrew to Germany. 1./JG 53 returned to the Channel Front at the start of April 1941, now flying Bf 109F-2s and defending against an RAF on the offensive, recording just one combat: a dogfight with Spitfires on 26 April 1941. However, on 4 June 1941, JG 53 moved east in preparation for the invasion of the Soviet Union, eventually arriving at Krzewica in eastern Poland on the evening of 15 June 1941.

Barbarossa begins

By now, I./JG 53 was commanded by Oblt Wilfried Balfanz (who had been wounded with Stab I./JG 51 on 14 May 1940 and subsequently joined Stab/JG 51), which had taken command at the start of June 1941 and had already shot down seven aircraft with JG 51. 2./JG 53 was commanded by the experienced Oblt Ignaz Prestele (who had seven kills to date) and 3./JG 53 by Oblt Werner Ursinius who, as yet, had no kills to his name.

Uffz Ludwig Riebel (right).

Barbarossa began early for Ohly on 22 June 1941. Taking off at 0340hrs, 1./JG 53 was tasked with escorting Stukas and he reported no contact with Soviet fighters. Landing an hour and ten minutes later, his Bf 109F-2 was refuelled and he took off again at 0630hrs on a fighter sweep, again reporting no contact with enemy aircraft but managing to shoot up a train instead. However, one from his Staffel, Uffz Ludwig Reibel, reported shooting down a Polikarpov I-153 biplane fighter near Brest Litovsk, the first kill of the offensive for I./JG 53 (and Reibel's second of the war, his first being a Blenheim on 14 May 1940). Landing again at 0743hrs, Ohly was airborne again at 0910hrs on another Stuka escort mission, reporting that Lt Walter Zellot from his Staffel had shot down a Polikarpov I-16, Zellot's first kill of the war.

It would then appear that 1./JG 53 flew another sortie without Ohly in command as Lt Ernst-Albrecht Schulz shot down three Tupolev SB-2s in quick succession (taking his score so far in the war to seven) and Ludwig Reibel shot another two SB-2s. Ohly was airborne again at 1218hrs, presumably on an alarmstart or scramble to intercept attacking Soviet aircraft as the flight only lasted 24 minutes, and he was pleased to report in his logbook that he shot down one SB-2 and badly damaged a second, which was later confirmed as destroyed. In the same flight, new pilot Fw Eckardt Wenzel also shot down an SB-2.

The day was not over for 1./JG 53 as, at 1630hrs, Ohly got airborne again on another Stuka escort mission, recording kills for Lt Udo Padior (an Ilyushin DB-3, which was his first kill of the war) and another for Fw Eckardt Wenzel near Biala-Podlaska. By the time Ohly landed at 1730hrs, he had flown five operational flights on the first day of *Barbarossa*, totalling five hours and two minutes. I./JG 53 claimed 18 aircraft without loss.

23 June 1941 was much quieter for I./JG 53, with the Gruppen Kommandeur Wilfried Balfanz claiming the only kill of the day (a Petlyakov Pe-2). Ohly had to turn back because of engine trouble on two missions and then, having changed aircraft, he had to turn back due to a faulty radio. He would fly a test flight of his 'White 7' that evening, reporting that the engine was working as it should; he was therefore airborne in the same aircraft at 0835hrs the following day.

The next day would be another quiet one for 1./JG 53, but the squadron would see its first casualty while attacking a formation of SB-3s (where six were claimed shot down) east of Pruzana. Gruppen Kommandeur Oblt Wilfried Balfanz was reported missing; leadership of the Gruppe was now given temporarily to Ignaz Prestelle while a new Gruppen Kommandeur was identified.

On the move

The afternoon of 25 June 1941 saw I./JG 53 moving eastwards to a new airfield at Pruzana from where Ohly flew an uneventful mission that evening. The following morning, he flew another sortie without incident. However, his evening's mission was far more notable, with Ohly, Ernst-Albrecht Schulz and Uffz Alfred Baumer each claiming an I-15 in the vicinity of Sluzk, as well as Ohly destroying another on the ground.

The pace of battle then eased off slightly, with just one flight for Ohly on 27 and 28 June 1941. 29 June 1941 saw two uneventful flights, the second being in the Minsk area, albeit on another mission that evening in which Ohly did not take part; Ernst-Albrecht Schulz shot down his ninth aircraft of the war, an SB-3 near Borisow. I./JG 53 then moved further east first to Baranowice on 29 June and then to Hostynne on 30 June 1941. During the course of the last move, 1./JG 53 suffered its first casualty of *Barbarossa* when Uffz Alfred Baumer was injured when he collided with another Bf 109 F-2.

It was then that the new Gruppen Kommandeur arrived, fresh from escaping from captivity. Hptm Franz von Werra had been shot down over southern England on 5 September 1940 while flying with Stab II./JG 3. After a number of well-documented escapes, he finally made it to the USA from Canada on 2 January 1941and arrived back in Germany in mid-April 1941 where he received the Ritterkreuz.

Ohly makes no mention of his new Gruppen Kommandeur's arrival and was more irritated by his Bf 109F-2's engine troubles. 'The engine has to be changed!', he angrily wrote on 1 July. The day after, 1 Staffel suffered its first combat casualty when Ernst-Albrecht Schulz was wounded attacking an SB-3. Schulz had joined 1./JG 53 in September 1939 and his wounds kept him out of action until early 1942.

The days that followed saw Ohly flying up to four sorties a day on a mixture of duties: escort, fighter sweeps and even, on 9 July, low-level attacks on Soviet tanks. I./JG 53 didn't increase its number of victories until 6 July (by which time it was flying from Dubno) with 11 aircraft claimed, one each to Lts Walter Zellot and Heinz Ryba of 1 Staffel. The following day, Franz von Werra started to increase his tally of five kills, achieved with II./JG 3, when he shot down a DB-3 near Ploskirow.

For Ohly, increasing his score eluded him: while attacking two aircraft on 9 July, his guns jammed and on 10 July 1941 (by which time they were operating from Miropol), he had to return early when his Rottenflieger, Lt Norbert Schäfer, suffered engine problems. On a mission that afternoon, Ohly noted they had operated as far as Shitomir and that Lt Walter Zellot shot down an SB-3. The following day would be more eventful. They flew three sorties, which saw Walter Zellot claiming two SB-3s and Heinz Ryba one. However, the following mission, which took off at 1555hrs, saw Heinz Ryba failing to return. His loss was avenged on the next sortie that evening when escorting He 111s – Walter Zellot and Udo Padior badly damaged two I-16s.

For the remaining weeks of July 1941, I./JG 53 would continue moving east, first to Shitomir and then to Bela-Zerkow. Losses would be light, although on shooting down his first aircraft, Lt Norbert Schäfer was forced to crash-land north-east of Zwishel when his fighter was hit in its cooling system and he was taken prisoner; eight and a half years later he returned to Germany. The only successful 1 Staffel pilots during this time were Walter Zellot (who claimed his 12th kill on 5 August 1941), Lt Udo Padior and Fw Eckardt Wenzel (who each shot down their third aircraft

Right: Lt Norbert Schäfer of 1./JG 53.

Below left: Captured I-153s.

Below right: Captured I-16.

on 29 July) and newcomer Oblt Hans-Joachim Heinecke, who had moved across from Stab I./JG 53 and achieved his 15th kill (his third with 1./JG 53) on 2 August 1941. During this time, Ohly noted that his beloved White 7 had been damaged in combat with Soviet fighters on 23 July 1941, and on 29 July he finally achieved his 11th kill: a DB-3 at 1705hrs near Smola. This was followed by his 12th kill on 2 August 1941 when he shot down an I-16 near Nowo Mirgorod at 1705hrs.

However, following the loss of Oblt Kurt Sochatzky, who was shot down and captured on 4 August 1941, Ohly moved across to take command of Sochatzky's 7./JG 3, which was also based at Bela-Zerkow. Ohly would fly just four more sorties with 1./JG 53 before handing over to Hans-Joachim Heinecke, Ohly flying his first mission with his new unit on 6 August 1941. Meanwhile, I./JG 53 started moving back to Germany the same day for rest and recuperation, handing over its aircraft to JG 3.

Back to training

Hans Ohly would remain with 7./JG 3 until 28 August 1942, during which time he shot down another four aircraft (an SB-3 on 11 August 1941; an I-16 on 19 September 1941, which was not confirmed; a Pe-2 on 4 October 1941; and another Pe-2 on 23 May 1942). In September 1942 he was then posted to 1/Ergänzungsgruppe Süd as an instructor and, in October 1942, he took command of the training unit 4./Jagdgruppe Ost. From October 1943 to the end of the war, he was at Luftkriegsschule 3. He would suffer a minor wound during an air raid on 30 May 1944 and would be promoted to major just before the war's end. He passed away in Frankfurt in 1998.

Having flown operationally from December 1939 until 28 August 1942, Ohly had been lucky to have only been shot down once (and on his second operational flight at that). Unlike many other Luftwaffe fighter pilots on the Russian Front, he did not amass a great number of kills, but he was lucky to survive unscathed. Franz von Werra, *The One that Got Away*, as his biography was titled, was killed in an accident when his Bf 109F-4 crashed in the North Sea due to engine failure on 25 October 1941, while Ohly's replacement, Hans-Joachim Heinecke, was wounded in 1942 but survived the war having achieved 28 kills; he passed away in 1990.

Above: SB-2.

Left: Lt Ernst-Albrecht Schulz seen here later in the war. He would be 1./JG 53's first combat casualty of *Barbarossa* being wounded on 2 July 1941.

Bf 109F-2s of II./JG 53. In the centre is the aircraft of Kommandeur Hptm Heinz Bretnütz.

Above left: Bretnütz (centre, facing camera with sunglasses) was shot down on 22 June 1941 after having shot down his 37th aircraft; he would die of his wounds five days later.

Above right: Lt Heinrich von Schwerdtner of 2./JG 53 after shooting down his first aircraft on 27 June 1941.

Above left: Hptm Franz von Werra, the new Gruppen Kommandeur.

Above right: Bf 109F-2 of II./JG 53 having moved from the Eastern Front to Holland in October 1941.

Chapter 11
Messerschmitt Me 210/410 Hornisse

The Me 210 and its successor, the Me 410, were intended to replace the Bf 110 but development of the Me 210 was fraught with problems to such an extent that the Bf 110 soldiered on until the end of the war, and the Me 410 was late into frontline service.

Me 210

The origins of the Me 210/410 go back to 1936 when the RLM drew up requirements for a replacement for the Bf 110 capable of carrying a 1,000kg bomb, having a dive bombing capability and better defensive armament. As a result of a proposal from Messerschmitt, an order for 2,000 aircraft was given to the company in autumn 1938, despite no prototypes having been flown or even a design agreed. When a design was forwarded, it was revolutionary in that Rheinmetall-Borsig and AEG had come up with electrically operated twin MG 131s located in two barbettes on both sides of the fuselage. Then, since the twin rudders had worked well on the Bf 110, they were retained on the first prototypes of what was designated the Me 210, but as the guns were mounted laterally, a single-rudder model was also tested. A bomb bay was located beneath the fuselage while the recessed nose gave the pilot better visibility during dive bombing missions; the aircraft was powered by Daimler-Benz DB 601A engines.

The first Me 210 prototype flew on 2 September 1939, but it was immediately clear that the fuselage had to be lengthened by a metre and that handling along the vertical axis was not very good. The second prototype then flew on 10 October 1939; it was still fitted with a double rudder but the single-rudder configuration became standard from the fifth prototype onwards. However, optimism was soon dashed when, on 5 September 1940, the horizontal stabiliser failed on the second prototype when the pilot pulled out of a 650kph dive and was forced to bale out. As a result, the fuselage of the third prototype was strengthened, which then added more weight to the aircraft. Soon after, more problems occurred when

Above left: Me 210V13, which was later converted to be an Me 410.

Above right: Me 210 being trialled at Rechlin, 1942.

it was found the Me 210 would stall when banking steeply (something the aircraft would have to do on almost every landing), and there was a problem with the undercarriage. Further development was needed between December 1940 and summer 1941, which meant trials did not restart until October 1941. During this period, the Luftwaffe began to make alternative employment plans for the Me 210, such as it being tropicalised and being used as a night-fighter, all of which further added to the delay.

In autumn 1941, a few aircraft were delivered to Erprobungsstaffel Me 210 (the Me 210 test and development unit) and I./SKG 210 (the unit originally designed to operate the Me 210 and which then became I./ Zerstörergeschwader 1 [I./ZG 1]). However, with 30 aircraft suffering training accidents of varying severity, in March 1942 it was agreed the Me 210 in its current form was too much of a danger to its crews. In addition to the flat-spin problem, there were instances of engines breaking loose in flight and aircraft flipping over on their backs, killing the crews. Messerschmitt was then informed that the Me 210 had been cancelled but that the current production of 240 Me 210s was to be finished first. Those Me 210s planned for frontline service would be replaced by other aircraft, but developmental work on the Me 210 project would continue. Any decision to resume production of the Me 210 would not be made until the fuselage was lengthened and balanced elevators and wing slats had been installed

On 1 May 1942, the final word on further production was expected. By then, six aircraft would have been modified, an autopilot installed and the aircraft would be configured as a Zerstörer or heavy fighter. On 27 April 1942, Oberstleutnant Edgar Petersen from the Luftwaffe test centre at Rechlin sent the first test report, which was positive and praised the improved stability. Petersen recommended that none of the airframes should be scrapped in light of the positive news and if further testing of the landing gear also proved successful, the aircraft could be declared suitable for operations as a high-speed bomber.

As a result, in July 1942 Erprobungsstaffel Me 210 (re-designated 16./Kampfgeschwader 6 (16./KG 6) in September 1942) began operational trials (albeit with mixed results) while, in October 1942, a number of modified Me 210A-1s went to III./ZG 1 and operated from Sicily (and would be joined by aircraft from 16./KG 6 at the end of the same month). III./ZG 1 continued operating the Me 210 until early summer 1943, when a new aircraft arrived as a replacement: the Me 410 Hornisse (Hornet).

The Hornet lands

In September of 1942 the designation 'Me 410' appeared more frequently in official documents. This was essentially the modified version of the Me 210, with the DB 603 engine. Oberstleutnant Petersen promised that 210 Me 410s with the DB 603 (as opposed to the Me 210's DB 601 engine) would be delivered by 1 December 1942 and used as day bombers against England. However, there was still debate as to the primary role for the Me 410. A high-speed bomber took primacy but with things changing for the Germans, a high-speed Zerstörer was equally attractive.

On 8 December 1942, the first of five Me 410s were delivered on schedule but the Allied bomber offensive during 1943 soon forced a shift to the defence of the Reich, as the Luftwaffe needed fighters, be they single- or twin-seaters. In January 1943, Erprobungsstaffel Me 410 was formed at Lechfeld to start developing the Me 410 for operations. Then, in June 1943, the Do 217 unit II./KG 40 began to convert to the Me 410, being re-designated V./KG 2, after which it began flying bombing missions over Britain, suffering its first loss on the night of 13 July 1943 to a Mosquito of 85 Sqn during an attack on Cambridge. V./KG 2 would continue flying bomber and intruder missions until June 1944, by which time it had been re-designated II./KG 51 and had been joined by I./KG 51. After a brief period of action over the Normandy beaches, operating in the bombing, intruding and even night-fighter roles, both Me 410 Gruppe were withdrawn to Germany for conversion to the Me 262.

At the same time, III./ZG 1, formerly flying Me 210s but now being prepared for Me 410s, was being considered for U-boat protection in the Mediterranean and Bay of Biscay (III./ZG 1 would become a Ju 88 C-6/R-2 unit in October 1943) while trials were carried out fitting the Me 410 with modified 5cm (BK 5) anti-tank guns in order to turn the Me 410 into a powerfully armed bomber destroyer. Despite this indicating an emphasis on the destroyer version, the breakdown of aircraft produced during 1943 still pointed to the bomber version – 200 bombers, 80 reconnaissance and 100 heavy fighters were built that year.

Defence of the Reich soon became a top priority and production now called for 280 aircraft per month by the end of 1944, with Bf 110 being used for night fighting and the Me 410 for day. Accordingly, new Me 410 variants now appeared. The initial version was the Me 410A-1, which was designed as a light bomber with fixed forward-firing machine guns and cannon, two rearward firing remotely controlled cannon and an internal bomb load of two 500kg bombs. The A-1/U1 was an armed photo-recce version, the A-1/U2 a heavy fighter and the A-1/U4 a bomber destroyer (with 5cm cannon). These were further improved with the A-2 (destroyer), A-3 (reconnaissance), B-1 (bomber), B-2 (destroyer with a pair of 30mm cannon) and B-3 (reconnaissance). Aircraft also carried underwing 21cm mortars or rockets. Later experimental types would be the B-5 (torpedo dropping with Hohentwiel maritime patrol radar) and B-6 (anti-shipping and similar to the B-5 but not fitted for torpedo dropping).

However, it is for daylight anti-bomber fighter missions that the Me 410 is better known, albeit its impact was minimal as it only served with ZG 26 and ZG 76, both units then being re-designated as single-seat fighter units from August to September 1944 onwards. One pilot was Oblt Fritz Stehle of II./ZG 26, who had started flying Bf 110s with 2./ZG 2 before going on to fly Me 210s with 8./ZG 1 and then Me 410s with 5./ZG 26. He relates what it was like attacking bombers:

> You really had to work hard on those bombers; it was very seldom that you knocked one down with the first burst. Sometimes you would sit behind a bomber and fire off all your ammunition into it and it would not move; it would just keep going.
>
> We fired rockets either in pairs or singly usually from behind the bomber formation. Sometimes the rockets were useful. As we ran into attack one could note a certain nervousness in the American bomber formation, the individual bombers started to go up and down relative to each other but aiming was difficult. Not only was it difficult to judge the range but the weapon was not very accurate in line. It was only of real value as a means of splitting up the enemy formations and sometimes it was successful in doing that.

Stehle would go on to shoot down 18 bombers including a number using the BK 5 cannon. He recalls how effective this gun was:

> In the windscreen we had a telescopic sight which had marks etched onto it to indicate the wing span of a B-17 at different ranges. The ideal engagement range was one km. After each firing the cannon took some seconds to re-load before it was ready to fire the next round. The rotary magazine carried some 21 rounds and each time the pneumatic reloading system went into operation you could hear the hiss of the compressed air above the engine noise.
>
> When you fired one round you might see it go above the bomber so you corrected and fired again and you might see the round go below the target. You then corrected a bit more and fired and you might see the round going towards the bomber then disappearing against the bomber's silhouette. Then you could relax because you knew that if you didn't see the shell any more, very soon it was going to hit the bomber. One two occasions I hit bombers when they still had bombs on board. When that happened there would be a great explosion and nothing more would be left of the bomber apart from the wingtips and tail.

By 1944, there were other problems and priorities on the horizon. The Luftwaffe ordered the He 177 bomber output to be increased from 100 to 200 per month and, as a result, some programmes had to be reduced. The Me 110 and the Me 410 were on the top of the list for being reduced and on 30 June 1944 Hitler ordered an increase in single-engine fighter production. As a result, 20 aircraft types, including the Me 210 and the Me 410, were cancelled. Furthermore, Me 410 losses to American fighters would soon dry up the pool of available Me 410s. For example, on 6 March 1944, 16 Bf 110s and Me 410s were shot down while attacking bombers and then, on 11 April 1944, eight Me 410s and three Bf 110s were shot down by American fighters; again, Fritz Stehle recalls what it was like:

> When we reached the bombers we would try to attack as soon as possible before the escorts could get onto us. Usually we did not have a fighter unit assigned to escorting the Me 410s to keep off the American escorts. Everybody was ordered to go for the bombers.
>
> When the Mustangs caught us it was terrible. Always we had to look behind ourselves for them. The Me 410 was useless in a dogfight as it couldn't turn well. It was too heavy and not manoeuvrable enough.

Above left and above right: Me 210A-1s being operationally tested with III./ZG 1 in North Africa, 1942–43.

If you were attacked by a Mustang you could only pray and hope your gunner shot well. My gunner Uffz Alois Slaby was very experienced and knew exactly when the fighter was about to fire. He would say "Not yet, not yet-NOW!" and I would chop the throttles and the Me 410 would decelerate very rapidly. If we were lucky the fighter would go screaming past us or sometimes I put the 410 into a skid with wings level and bullets would flash past the wing tip. We knew that if we could buy a little time that often meant survival.

With production of the Me 410 finished by summer 1944 and those units disbanded, the Me 410 only remained in service with a limited number of reconnaissance units and the air-sea rescue unit Seenotgruppe 80.

Hungary was the only other German ally that operated the Me 210, where it was made under licence with half the production being shipped to Germany and the other half retained by the Hungarians. Unsurprisingly, the Hungarians experienced the same problems as the Germans, albeit some Me 210s were still being used in the fast bomber role against the Soviets at the end of the war.

Although a number of Me 410s were captured during and after the war, only two still exist. At the RAF Museum Collection in Cosford, there is an Me 410A-1/U2, Wk Nr 420430, which is marked as 3U+AK of 2./ZG 26 (with the factory code PD+VO; this was from 3 (Fern)/Aufklärungsgruppe 122 (3.F)/122). It was captured at Vaerløse, Denmark, in 1945. Undergoing restoration in the USA is Me 410 A-3, 10018 coded F6+WK of 2.(F)/122. Two more examples, Me 410A-3, Wk Nr 10259 coded F6+OK of 2.(F)/122 captured at Montecorvino on 26 November 1943, and Me 410B-6 10278 were also evaluated but were sadly scrapped.

Left: Me 410V1.

Below left: Me 410A-1 of V./KG 2, 1944.

Below right: Me 410A-1.

Above left: Me 410B-2/U1 with its increased armament.

Above right: Me 410s of ZG 26 showing the clog badge of II Gruppe.

Above and right: Me 410B-2 armed with four WG 21cm mortars.

Above left: Me 410 fitted with BK 5 cannon.

Above right: Me 410A-1/U4 of ZG 26 breaks away from attacking a B-17, 12 May 1944.

Above left and above right: Me 410B-6 fitted with the FuG Hohentwiel maritime patrol radar.

A Me 210 being operated by the Hungarian Air Force.

Chapter 12
Dornier's Twin-Engined Arrow

The Dornier Do 335 Pfeil (Arrow) was probably the most unusual single-seat fighter aircraft of World War Two in that it had a piston engine at either end of the fuselage, one pushing and one pulling. Had it become operational, it would have been the fastest piston-engined fighter in service at that time.

Origins

Dr Claude Dornier had already designed aircraft with push and pull engines, namely the 12-engined Do X flying boat and the Dornier Wal and Super Wal. In 1941, Dr Ulrich Hütter designed the Göppingen Gö 9 – a scaled-down version of the Do 17 with a Hirth HM 60 engine, which was located in the fuselage, powering an airscrew at the rear of the aircraft, which would push it forward. Testing of this unusual aircraft was positive, which gave Dornier the impetus to design an aircraft with a propeller at the front and rear of the fuselage. At the outbreak of war, Dornier had been working on the P.59 high-speed tandem-engine bomber. However, in early 1940, work stopped to concentrate on other types such as the Do 217 bomber. Then, in May 1942, Dornier submitted a design for the P.231 single-seat intruder, which was capable of carrying a 2,200lb (1000g) bomb load, and despite competition from other German aircraft manufacturers, Dornier was awarded the contract for what would be called the Do 335. However, that autumn, the RLM decided it did not need a bomber, so the Do 335 was redesigned as a fighter. The aircraft would now be powered by two DB 603 engines, and the first prototype (Do 335V1 coded CP+UA) took to the air on 26 October 1943. A series of minor issues with the aircraft followed, which had to be sorted before the Do 335V2 CP+UB got airborne on 31 December 1943. This aircraft was powered by two up-rated DB 603A-2 engines, while the Do 335V3 (CP+UC), which emerged three weeks later, would be powered by DB 603G-0 engines. The V2 would crash at Memmingen on 15 April 1944 when test pilot and engineer Werner Altrogge lost control testing the roll characteristics of the Do 335 after the engine failed; he was killed when his ejection seat failed to work correctly. As with a number of German aircraft introduced later in the war, it was intended that the Do 335 be fitted with an ejection seat; in an emergency, the pilot could detonate explosive bolts and jettison the pusher airscrew and dorsal fin and, when fired, the pneumatic ejection seat pushed the pilot away from the aircraft.

Into production too late

Undeterred, the RLM now placed initial orders, as flight testing had revealed the Do 335 had potentially good handling characteristics, and it was fast. At least 16 prototypes flew, during which armament of two 15mm MG 151 cannon were fitted on top of the front engine, a 30mm MK 103 cannon firing through the centre of the spinner and, later, another MK 103 cannon could be fitted on each of the wings. This resulted in ten pre-production Do 335A-0s being delivered for testing in May 1944, by which time Hitler had announced the Emergency Fighter Programme, part of which gave priority to the Do 335, and, in late 1944, the Do 335 started to be produced. However, a bombing raid on Friedrichshafen-Manzel in March 1944, where the Do 335 was to be produced, caused delays when much of the tooling was destroyed or damaged. The first Do 335s were not completed until January 1945 and when the factory at Oberpfaffenhofen was captured in April 1945, just 11 Do 335A-1 fighter-bombers had been completed, while up to eight Do 335A-11 two-seat trainers had been completed or were under construction.

In December 1944, four Do 335s had been assigned to Erprobungskommando 335 at Mengen, the unit formed to operationally test the Do 335. On 24 December 1944, Feldwebel Alfred Wollank was killed when Do 335V4 Wk Nr 230004 CP+UD crashed at Bonefeld near Koblenz on a transfer flight from Oberpfaffenhofen to Rechlin. It was assumed that during a day of massive air activity over Germany, he had been shot down by an American escort fighter, but there are no claims or reports that would appear to support this. This unit was disbanded in February 1945 and it has been suggested that JG 26 would be equipped with the Do 335 as, on 26 March 1945, Oblt Heinrich Schild of 12./JG 26, who was recovering from wounds received on 12 October 1944 when his Bf 109G-14 had been shot down by American fighters, test flew Do 335V9 at Rechlin. Flt Lt Pierre Clostermann of 3 Sqn, flying a Hawker Tempest, claims to have encountered a Do 335 in combat towards the end of April 1945, but no mention of this was made in the squadron ORB. Other records state that Lt Randolph Cooper of the 357th Fighter Sqn/355 Fighter Ground damaged a Do 335 in combat on 4 April 1945, but subsequent research identified his opponent as a Me 262.

Above left and left: Do 335V1.

Above right: Do 335V11.

Cancellation

Erprobungskommando 335 was disbanded in mid-February 1945 and a number of Do 335s were captured at Oberpfaffenhofen at the end of the war. The RAF were given two by the Americans – the first was a Do 335A-0 believed to be Wk Nr 240016, which was damaged in an accident at Merville on 13 December 1945 and never recovered to the UK. The second was a Do 335A-11 Wk Nr 240112 RP+UB, but on 18 January 1946, while being flown by Gp Capt Alan Hards DSO, Commanding Officer of the Royal Aircraft Establishment, the rear engine caught fire and the elevator controls were burnt through, after which the Do 335 crashed into Cove Junior School near Farnborough, killing the pilot and injuring six on the ground. The French Air Force obtained two, possibly three, aircraft, two of which were Do 335M14 Wk Nr 230014 RP+UQ and M17 Wk Nr 240313. Both were scrapped in 1949. The Americans also captured a number of aircraft, of which Do 335A-02 Wk Nr 240102 VG+PH has survived and is currently on display at the Steven F Udvar-Hazy Centre, Chantilly, Virginia.

Above left: Do 335A-0 Wk Nr 240107.

Above right: Do 335 two-seat trainer. This aircraft crashed near Farnborough on 18 January 1946.

Do 335 being evaluated by the French Air Force at Brétigny, 1948.

Chapter 13
The Weird and the Wonderful

Throughout the war, the Luftwaffe tried to come up with better fighters to counter the improving Allied aircraft they were up against. Most of these were either abandoned or arrived on the front line too late to go into combat.

Messerschmitt Me/Blohm Und Voss BV 155

A Royal Aircraft Establishment (RAE) report dated November 1946 titled 'Foreign Aircraft-Blohm und Voss 155B General Examination' describes this aircraft as:

> A single-seat, single-engine (Daimler-Benz 603 U) high-altitude fighter. It has a maximum speed of 431mph between 51,000 and 53,000ft and a ceiling of 56,000ft and is armed with two 20mm and one 30mm guns. The design is believed to be based on a former Messerschmitt Project which was handed over to Blohm und Voss for development. The outer wings and rear fuselage a closely reminiscent of the Me 109. The take-off weight with 110 gallons of fuel is 12,320lb giving a wing loading of 29.3lb/sq.ft. The wing span is 67 ft.

Again designed as a high-altitude interceptor to counter the threat of the B-29, it was based on Messerschmitt's design for the Me 155 carrier-borne fighter. However, since the carrier *Graf Zeppelin* never became operational, in November 1942 Messerschmitt began redesigning it to be a fast fighter-bomber. As there was then no requirement for what they called the Me 155A, in August 1943 prototype construction of a high-altitude interceptor was about to commence when the RLM ordered Blohm und Voss to take over further development, the aircraft now being called the BV 155B as opposed to Me 155B; the RLM placed an order for five prototypes, the first of which flew on 8 February 1945. Two more prototypes were built but the end of the war put a stop to any further testing or development. The BV 155V2 Wk Nr 360052 was

Above left: Me 155/BV 155.

Above right: Walter and Reimar Horten, the designers of the Ho 229.

captured in a semi-completed condition at Hamburg-Finkenwerder, shipped to the RAE for evaluation and exhibition, after which it was shipped to America. It was evaluated at Wright Field, Ohio, and eventually transferred (bearing Foreign Equipment Number FE-505) to the National Air and Space Museum, Washington, DC. Most sources claimed this was the unfinished V3 prototype, but in 1998, while reassembling parts stored at the Paul E Garber Facility in Silver Hill, Maryland, nearly the entire airframe was discovered. Except for wiring harnesses, which were never hooked up in the BV, and some other small parts, the aircraft appeared to be 90–95% complete, including most of the propulsion system. German documents verify that the V3 was only half-finished at war's end and the discovery of 'V2' stamped into both sides of the windshield frame seems to prove that this aircraft is the second prototype.

Me 209.

Horten Ho IV/ 229

Probably the most unique and advanced potential fighter aircraft of World War Two was the distinctive flying wing designed by Walter and Reimar Horten (a third brother, Oblt Wolfram Horten, was reported missing while flying an He 111 of 1./Kampfgruppe 126 off Boulogne on 21 May 1940). Walter was a pre-war fighter pilot who had an engineering background and because of which, in December 1939, he became the Geschwader Technischer Offizier for JG 26. He shot down two aircraft on 28 August 1940, claiming two Boulton Paul Defiants, and his seventh and final victory came on 30 September 1940. He was then posted to the RLM in May 1941. However, before the war, the brothers had designed a series of tailless all-wing gliders. Their initial design was the Horten Ho IV tailless flying wing glider, in which the pilot lay on his front in a prone position, thus helping to reduce drag. Four of these were built in Göttingen between 1941 and 1943, but in 1943, and with the war turning against Germany, the RLM wanted proposals for a bomber that could carry a 1,000kg bomb load over 1,000km at 1,000kph – a very demanding request. It was thought that the Jumo 004B turbojets would achieve much of this (albeit the engine had high fuel consumption). The Hortens proposed that their flying wing design, with minimal modification and powered by suitable engines, could possibly meet this and in August 1943 work began on what would be the Horten IX, with the Hortens leading what was called Luftwaffe Kommando IX.

The Ho IX had a centre section made from welded steel tubing and wing spars built from wood. The wings were made from two thin carbon-impregnated plywood panels glued together with a mixture of charcoal and sawdust. The wing had a single main spar, penetrated by the jet engine inlets. The aircraft had a retractable tricycle landing gear. However, it was now decided that this aircraft should be fitted with two 30mm cannon and for it to be a fighter not a bomber. The first flight of the Ho IX V1, an unpowered glider, was in March 1944 and results were good only for the aircraft to be damaged in an accident, after which it went to the Gothaer Waggonfabrik for modification and repair. The Ho IX V2 was then fitted with Jumo 004 engines and despite it not flying until the start of February 1945, Gothaer Waggonfabrik was instructed to construct 40 aircraft (in two batches of 20) to be designated the Go 229. Trials, especially in combat against the Me 262, went well but then, on 18 February 1945, one of the engines caught fire during a flight test and it crashed at Oranienburg, killing test pilot Lt Erwin Ziller, who was a pre-war professional glider pilot instructor and mid-1943 was with Erprobungsstelle Rechlin.

Undeterred, work now accelerated for the Ho IX V3 at the factory at Friedrichroda. It would be larger, be armed with two MK 108 30mm cannon and powered by the improved Jumo 004C. Work also began on V4 and V5 which would be two-seat night fighters and V6 (armaments test aircraft) and V7 (trainer) but before the V3 could fly, the factory at Friedrichroda was captured by American troops who, under Operation Paperclip, were then keen to obtain as much of Germany's advanced projects, especially before the Soviets could. As a result, four Horten gliders or parts of them exist in the USA (and two in Germany) while the Ho IX V3 is visible to the public inside the Mary Baker Engen Restoration Hangar at the Smithsonian National Air and Space Museum's Steven F Udvar-Hazy Centre, Chantilly, Virginia. Some sources refer to this aircraft as the Gotha Go or Ho 229 but even the Horten brothers after the war refer to it as the Horten 229.

Messerschmitt ME 209/309

It was inevitable that, buoyed by the success of the Bf 109, Messerschmitt would look at successors. Design of the Me 209 began in 1937 and it first flew on 1 August 1938. It was designed as a single-engined high-speed aircraft using surface evaporation cooling instead of drag-inducing radiators. It was powered by an up-rated DB 601 R engine and on 26 April 1939, in the hands of test pilot Fritz Wendel, Me 209V1 coded D-INJR broke the piston-engined world speed record. A second prototype (D-IVFP) crashed in April 1939, just eight weeks after its first flight. A third prototype (D-IVFP) was completed in May 1939, but it was the fourth and final prototype (D-IRND) that was intended to be a fighter. Basic armament would be two MG 17s on the top of the cowling and possibly a cannon firing through the propeller hub. However, this resulted in poorer performance compared to the Bf 109E-4, so further work was abandoned. The fuselage of the Me 209V1 is still in existence in the Muzeum Lotnictwa I Astronautyki, Kraków, Poland, but it is missing its wings and other major parts.

In 1943, Messerschmitt began work on a modernised, more powerful version of the Bf 109, with an inward-retracting undercarriage, a larger wing span, bigger tail and powered by the DB 603A engine. Unusually, it too was designated the Me 209 but bore more similarities with the Bf 109G and none with the original Me 209. From the start, it was destined to failure, mainly because it was up against the Fw 190D-9 and Ta 142. Furthermore, the DB 603 engines were in short supply, so the Me 209 had to use the less powerful Jumo 213 engine, which necessitated modifications to the cowling and cooling system. The Me 209V5 (sometimes known as the Me 209-II) first flew in November 1943, followed by the Jumo 213-powered Me 209V6 a few weeks later. Performance of the V5 was good and it was intended to be armed with a single MK108 firing through the propeller hub, with two 13mm machine guns in the wing root. However, compared to the Fw 190D-9, which was about to come into service, the Me 209 was

Above left: **Me 309.**

Above right: **Me 263/Ju 248.**

clearly inferior, so further development was cancelled.

Finally, the Me 209-II was predated by the Me 309, a direct replacement for the Bf 109E and F. Powered by a DB 603A engine and fitted with a tricycle undercarriage, the Me 309V1 (GE+CU) began taxiing trials in June 1942 but immediately encountered problems with its undercarriage. Then the first test flight, on 18 July 1942, lasted a mere five minutes as the engine temperature rose alarmingly and it suffered hydraulic problems, which resulted in undercarriage issues.

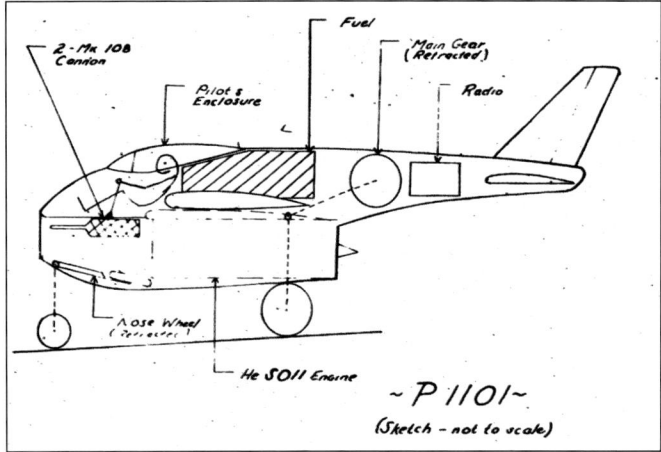

Schematic of the P.1101.

Subsequent test flights proved that the V1 suffered from instability and when that was sorted out, it was found to be inferior to the Bf 109G – the aircraft it was intended to replace. A second prototype crashed on its first test flight but development continued. The engine was changed to a DB 605, the third prototype incorporated further modifications, while the fourth prototype, which first flew in July 1943, was fitted with two wing-mounted MK 108 cannon, two MG 131 and two MG 151 cannon in the wing roots and two MG 131 in the fuselage. However, like the Me 209-II, it was inferior to the new Focke-Wulf fighters and further development was cancelled. There was a proposal to join two Me 309 fuselages together, similar to the American twin-Mustang, but this proposal was never developed.

Messerschmitt Me 263/Junkers Ju 248

The Me 263 was another rocket-powered fighter and based on the Me 163C, which was powered by the HWK 509 series of engines. However, like the Me 155, the RLM ordered Messerschmitt AG to hand over design and development to Junkers Flugzeug und Motorenwerke AG. Junkers then came up with a pressurised cockpit, bigger fuel tanks and a retractable, as opposed to a jettisonable, undercarriage and renamed the design Ju 248; this aircraft was named Flunder (Flounder), while the Me 263 was named Scholle (Plaice). However, in November 1944, the RLM changed the Ju 248 back to the Me 263, by which time the Me 263/Ju 248V1 had been completed. Unpowered flights took place in February 1945 by means of a tug aircraft, during which problems were discovered with its centre of gravity. However, by that stage of the war, fuel was scarce, Allied bombing made it difficult to continue design and development and Allied fighters made the skies above Germany dangerous for flight testing. In April 1945, American troops captured the three prototypes, of which one was destroyed. One was shipped to America and the other to the Soviets, who used it as the basis for their MiG I-270.

P-1101

Messerschmitt was given the task of developing a fighter, in addition to the Me 262, with better performance but the same endurance and range using an engine for which the fuel consumption could be substantially reduced with no reduction in its operational capability. The first project was the P-1101; it was rushed ahead without any consideration for what would be the best solution. The pilot would sit forward, with the fuel tank located above the engine; a two-metre-span model was tested successfully in a wind tunnel. However, the prototype, powered by a Jumo 002 engine (with the intention of it later being fitted with the He-S 011 engine), was complete at the end of the war but believed to have been blown up before the arrival of American troops at Oberammergau in southern Germany on 29 April 1945. However, photographs show American soldiers posing alongside a fuselage with the inscription 'Me P-1101V1' on the nose. The P-1106 was similar to the P-1101 but the pilot would sit at the rear of the fuselage, and while the P-1110 and P-1111 were proposed, none were ever completed. The incomplete prototype and associated documents were shipped to America and, ultimately, to the Bell Aircraft Corporation – its Bell X-5, which flew on 20 June 1951, bore a remarkable resemblance to the P-1101.

Bachem BA 349 Natter

One of Germany's most spectacular projects was this relatively inexpensive semi-expendable rocket-powered point-defence interceptor. The Natter (which means Adder or Viper) would be launched vertically from a tower, then the pilot would fire the 24 x 73mm Föhn rocket shells stored in the nose at Allied bomber formations, before the pilot and fuselage (minus the disposable nose section) would return to earth on separate parachutes, allowing the aircraft to hopefully be used again.

Designer Erich Bachem proposed this radical aircraft which, apart from the engines, fuel tanks and autopilot, used non-essential materials for its construction. The wings, tail and fuselage were made of nailed and glued wood but the pilot was protected by an armoured windscreen and an armoured bulkhead. It was intended to power the interceptor with a Walter HWK 109-509A-2 rocket motor, which mixed hydrogen peroxide and water (T-Stoff) with hydrazine hydrate and methyl alcohol (C-Stoff) but only the A-1 version of the engine, which was also used by the in service Me 163, was readily available. Additional thrust for take-off would be given by four Schmidding SG34 solid fuel rocket boosters.

The tactic was that, after launch, the Natter would be guided towards its intended target by autopilot. Later versions were planned to have radar beam guidance to the autopilot system or a ground-to-air radio link. Only when close to the target would the pilot take full control, aim and launch the rockets and then dive away. When safe, he would bale out. It should be stressed that the Natter had no dogfighting ability.

The first prototype was completed 4 October 1944 and piloted glider flights, towed aloft by a tug aircraft, followed the next month. Uncrewed vertical take-off trials using only the Schmidding boosters started on 22 December 1944. By now, the SS had taken a personal interest in the Natter and had ordered production to go ahead at Bachem's Waldsee factory in southern Germany. Keen to get it into action, the SS and RLM pushed for a piloted flight. A flight with a dummy pilot and all rocket engines in place, therefore, occurred on 25 February 1945 and after a successful take-off, the nose separated, the dummy pilot was ejected safely and the fuselage descended as it should, only to be destroyed on hitting the ground when residual fuel exploded. Buoyed by this, on 1 March 1945, Oblt Lothar Sieber carried out the first piloted test from the site at the Ochsenkopf in southern Germany. Following a successful launch, control was lost – the cockpit was seen to fly off, after which the Natter continued to climb inverted, arched over. The Natter then pitched forward, hitting the ground near Nusplingen; very little was found of the unfortunate pilot. It is thought that Sieber had lost consciousness, probably as a result of being hit by the cockpit, which appeared to not have been locked correctly or had failed. Sieber was an interesting character: born in April 1922, he joined the Luftwaffe in November 1939 and, after training, it appears he was destined for transport or bomber aircraft only to be court martialled for failing to report for guard duty and then falsifying an entry in the guard duty book. He later appears to have joined 2./Versuchsverband ObdL, which became I./KG 200 in February 1944, with Sieber carrying out covert operations behind enemy lines.

Despite this setback, a further three test flights of an unmanned operational Natter were carried out, the third being completely successful; it was then decided to operationally evaluate the aircraft. Ten A-type aircraft were subsequently built for what was called Operation *Krokus* and three launch pads were built at Hasenholz near Holzmaden, south-west of Stuttgart. However, before they could go operational, American troops captured Holzmaden on 20 April 1945, forcing the evacuation of personnel to Waldsee, which itself was then captured by French troops on 26 April 1945.

Because of its uniqueness, a number of the 36 or so that were manufactured were captured and taken away for evaluation. However, only two original or partially original Natters are known to exist today. The Deutsches Museum in Munich displays a partially restored Natter in the colours and markings of one of the unmanned test aircraft, while the National Air and Space Museum in the USA has the only fully original Natter, which was captured in May 1945 and shipped to Freeman Field, Indiana, for analysis. The captured equipment number T2-1 was assigned to the Natter before it was transferred to the Silver Hill (later Paul E Garber) Smithsonian Collection in 1950. It is currently in storage at the Steven F Udvar-Hazy Center of the National Air and Space Museum.

Right and below: **Bachem Natter.**

Chapter 14
Messerschmitt's Swallow

The Messerschmitt Me 262, which acquired the nicknames Schnellbomber, Sturmvogel and Schwalbe (Fast bomber, Stormy Petrel (Storm Bird) and Swallow), was the world's first operational jet fighter, whose origins began a year before the outbreak of World War Two.

Emergence

The Me 262 first emerged from the drawing board as far back as October 1938 when project studies for a jet fighter designated P1065 began. Simultaneously, BMW was developing its P3302 gas turbine engines, engines which would, it hoped, produce over 1,300lb of thrust. In June 1939, the project was passed to the RLM, after which design and production moved ahead. As was usual with wartime German aircraft development, what initially slowed things down were the engines. BMW was over-optimistic as to the thrust from their engines and they were still a year late in having them bench tested.

The first flight of the P1065 did not take place until April 1941 and even then, it was powered by a nose-fitted piston engine. It was not until July 1941 that the first BMW P3302 engines were fitted (the engine now being designated the BMW 003) and in March 1942, the Messerschmitt test pilot, took the aircraft, now designated the Me 262, to the skies, albeit it still had the piston engine fitted, which was good thing as both jet engines flamed out. It was obvious that the BMW 003 was not yet fit for purpose but now Junkers had produced its Jumo 004 turbojet which produced 2,200lbs of thrust. These engines were fitted to the Me 262V3 and in July 1942, test pilot Fritz Wendel took off on the Me 262's first jet powered flight (the nose engine having at last been removed). The V3 was different to the later operational versions in that it was a 'tail dragger' – later versions would have a nose wheel as opposed to a tail wheel as the aircraft's centre of gravity was moved forward.

Me 262A-1 V167 prototype.

Me 262A-1a of III./EJG 2 under tow.

Early test flights showed that the Me 262 could reach speeds of 500mph but more problems now arose which would slow things down. The engines proved to be temperamental, engine production was slow and there were still those in the Luftwaffe who saw little value in such a plane – the Fw 190A and Bf 109G were superior tried and tested fighters that could operate from established airfields or rough airstrips, something which would hamper the Me 262. Nevertheless, small orders were placed in middle and late 1942 which was fortuitous as by spring 1943, it was obvious that Germany's war and especially the air war was starting to turn in the Allies' favour as they began to develop more superior fighters. It was now hoped that the Me 262 would help tip the balance back in Germany's favour.

Generalmajor Adolf Galland, the Inspector of Fighters, now intervened. Having flown the Me 262V4 in May 1943, he could see how the Me 262 could make a difference. Galland convinced Luftwaffe senior officers, and by early summer 1943, orders totalling 675 jets had been placed. However, the Me 262 was still undergoing development. V5 flew in July 1943 and was the first to be fitted with the more usual tricycle undercarriage, and then V6 was designated the pre-production prototype. Then, disaster struck – on 17 August 1943, the Messerschmitt plant at Regensburg was bombed by the USAAF, with over 400 workforce members killed, severe damage to the facilities and a number of production jigs destroyed. Like Supermarine, whose factory near Southampton was bombed in September 1940 resulting in dispersal of Spitfire production around the UK, Messerschmitt was forced to do the same. The attack and subsequent dispersal had a knock-on effect on production of the Me 262, and by early 1944, the Luftwaffe was even more desperate to get its hands on the jet. This is best summed up by Generalfeldmarschall Erhard Milch, who was in charge of aircraft production programmes. At a conference in Berlin in January 1944, he stated: 'We need the Me 262 before all else, before U-boats and tanks, because without this aircraft, armament production will no longer be possible.'

Despite these words, by the end of the same month, only Me 262V9 had flown; another 23 had been completed but were still waiting for engines, engines that Junkers was struggling to produce. It was not until April 1944 that the first Me 262A-1 (the primary production version) was completed and by the

Me 262A-1a of Erprobungskommando 262.

end of the month, another 15 had been delivered, with a further seven arriving the following month. At long last it was hoped that the Me 262 could be blooded.

Into action

On 19 April 1944, Erprobungskommando 262 (Ekdo 262) was formed at Lechfeld, commanded by Hptm Werner Thierfelder flying Me 262A-1a fighters, now nicknamed Schwalbe. The problem that now faced Thierfelder was, how would the Me 262 be used: fighter or bomber? Adolf Hitler had witnessed the jet being displayed in November 1943, which had convinced him that it should be used as a bomber, and the arguments for and against came to a head in May 1944 when Hitler had asked how the Me 262 was progressing as a bomber, only to be told that the Luftwaffe was developing it as a fighter. Hitler then flew into a rage, blaming all and sundry for incompetence, after which, aircraft coming off the production line found themselves primarily allocated to bomber units. Nevertheless, by the time of the Allied invasion of Normandy on 6 June 1944, only 30 or so Me 262s had been delivered.

Ekdo 262 continued to try and develop the fighter, suffering its first loss on 19 May 1944 when Uffz Kurt Flachs was killed in an accident. At the start of June 1944, elements of bomber unit Kampfgeschwader 51 (KG 51) were ordered to Lechfeld to convert to the Me 262 – proof that Hitler's rage had resulted in the Me 262 being used as a bomber. Furthermore, Einsatzkommando Braunegg, commanded by Hptm Herward Braunegg, had also been formed at Lechfeld to use the jet in the reconnaissance role.

It was still early days and Ekdo 262 struggled to get to terms with its task, which was not helped by the death of Werner Thierfelder on 18 July 1944. Apparently scrambled to intercept an air raid, he failed to return and his body was found in the wreckage of his Me 262. Command of Ekdo 262 then passed to Hptm Horst Geyer, another experienced fighter pilot.

It was not until 26 July 1944 that the first official combat occurred. A 544 Sqn Mosquito, flown by Flt Lt Bert Wall, with Plt Off Bert Lobban as his navigator, got airborne from RAF Benson in Oxfordshire on a sortie to Munich. At 29,000ft and in the target area, a twin-engined aircraft was spotted closing in fast, so the RAF pilot opened his throttles, confident of his escape. However, to his consternation, the German aircraft overtook them, then turned in behind them from astern. Wall broke hard to starboard but the enemy aircraft was quickly behind them again and opened fire from 800 yards. Wall broke hard again with the same result – the aircraft was quickly back behind them. This was repeated five more times before the enemy aircraft delivered a climbing attack from below, followed by a loud bang before the Mosquito successfully made it into cloud. Not sure what had caused the bang (probably a door breaking loose), the Mosquito headed for Italy, landing successfully. The damage inflicted was not recorded but Lt Alfred 'Bubi' Schreiber was credited with the first Me 262 kill, although, as it would appear, this was a little optimistic.

Me 262A-1 armed with 12 R4M rockets.

Trials continued but the flow of new aircraft was not helped by nine aircraft being destroyed or damaged in the bombing of the manufacturing plant at Leipheim on 19 July 1944, which reduced the flow from 59 in July to 20 in August 1944. However, at the end of August, it is believed the first bombing raids by Me 262s were carried out. 3./KG 51, led by Hptm Wolfgang Schenk, carried out sporadic attacks from altitude using Me 262A-2as, the bombers now being nicknamed Sturmvogel. The effectiveness of Kommando Schenk is uncertain as very few records exist to prove it one way or another; after just over a month later, the jets returned to be with I./KG 51 at Rheine.

The start of September 1944 saw a reorganisation of the Me 262 units. Einsatzkommando Braunegg would end up subordinated to Nahaufklärungsgruppe 6 and Ekdo 262 would be renamed Kommando Nowotny, after its highly successful and highly decorated commander, Maj Walter Nowotny. Kommando Nowotny had a nominal strength of 40 aircraft split between two Staffeln and based at Achmer and Hesepe. Allied air power was making things increasingly difficult for the Me 262 pilots but having been declared operational on 3 October 1944, the first kills came the following day when Hptm Georg-Peter Eder claimed two B-17s. The next day saw 401 Sqn claiming the first Me 262 when in an exciting combat, five Spitfires, led by Sqn Ldr Rod Smith, shot down Hptm Hans-Christof Büttmann of I./KG 51 near Nijmegen.

By now, combats with Me 262s were becoming increasingly commonplace. One of the methods of countering the jets was to place standing patrols over airfields attacking them as they came into land low on fuel. 'Rat catching', as it became known, was quite successful but became increasingly dangerous as the Germans increased flak defences to keep the Allied fighters away. It is believed that rat catching resulted in the death of Maj Walter Nowotny on 8 November 1944. The day was busy, with the German jets claiming to have shot down ten American fighters and bombers for the loss of three Me 262s. It is not clear what exactly happened to Nowotny but it is believed he was shot down by Lt Robert W Stevens of 364th Fighter Group, who attacked a jet near the Dummer Lake and shot it down at Ede. The cloud base was low and after hearing gunfire, an Me 262 was seen to emerge vertically from the cloud base and exploded a kilometre away from the airfield; Nowotny, who had just claimed his 258th kill, lost his life in the crash. The following day, Kommando Nowotny was withdrawn from operations to Lechfeld to form III./JG 7, which would be

A Me 262A-2 laden with two 250kg bombs.

commanded by Hptm Erich Hohagen. Training would now be carried out by Ergänzungs-Jagdgeschwader 2 (EJG 2), the operational Gruppe being III./EJG 2.

JG 7, commanded initially by Obstlt Johannes Steinhoff, was, in the main, operational with only III Gruppe. The first kill was credited to Hptm Georg-Peter Eder on 21 November 1944, I./JG 7 having to wait until 19 March 1945 for its first kill. At the same time, a number of new units sprang up, the most notable being Kommando Welter, named after Lt Kurt Welter. Flying the Me 262B-1a/U1 night-fighter, it was intended that the Me 262 would counter RAF Mosquitos, Welter scoring the first night kill for an Me 262 on 12 December 1944. The following month, his Kommando was renamed 10./Nachtjagdgeschwader 11. Other units also appeared, namely I/KG (J) 54 and KG (J) 6; these were originally bomber units and were being re-roled as fighters – they were operational for a short period with limited success.

A final unit was Jagdverband 44 (JV 44), the nucleus of which was made up by a plethora of highly decorated and experienced pilots led by Generalmajor Adolf Galland, now relieved of his post as Inspector of Fighters by Hermann Göring for disagreeing with him. JV 44 flew its first mission on 5 April 1945, claiming a number of American bombers, but by now it was too little too late. With the Allies enjoying air superiority, any Me 262 pilot would be harassed by Allied combat aircraft on the ground, on take-off, in combat and on landing, and a number would be wounded or killed in action, especially in the last month – Oblt Franz Schall (133 victories, killed 10 April), Maj Gerhard Barkhorn (301 victories, wounded 21 April), Oberst Günther Lützow (110 victories, killed 21 April) and Generalleutnant Adolf Galland (103 victories, wounded 26 April 1945) were just four notable casualties.

Grounded

About 1,400 Me 262s were produced, but the most that were operational simultaneously was between 180 and 200. As the war ended, Me 262s were found scattered all over Germany – on airfields, on motorway

Above left: The Me 262 was vulnerable. Having just shot down a P-51 Mustang of the 357th Fighter Group, Lt Franz Schall of Kommando Nowotny was shot down by another P-51, Quakenbrück, 8 November 1944. Schall baled out and went on to survive the war.

Above right: Me 262 B-1a/U1 of 10./NJG 11 captured by the RAF at the end of the war.

airstrips and in the process of rolling off production lines. A number of pilots even flew to neutral countries or British and American held airfields rather than falling into the hands of the Soviets.

Many Me 262s were found in flying condition and were quickly acquired by the Americans, British, French and Soviets, who used the technology to improve their own jet development. The Czechs even continued to build the Me 262 as the Avia S-92 (single seat) and the Avia CS-92 (twin seat). These jets served in operational units until 1951 when they were replaced by more modern Soviet aircraft.

As a result, original Me 262s can be found in museums around the world – in Germany (two), the USA (three), the UK (one), Australia (one) and South Africa (one), and in the Czech Republic, two Avias can be found in the Prague Aviation Museum. Parts of Me 262 wreckages are still being discovered. At the end of October 2014, the Dutch Air Force found the remains of an aircraft clearly identifiable as an Me 262, which turned out to be an A-2a, Wk Nr 130026 coded 9K+AL of 3/KG 51. This aircraft had been shot down by German flak on 12 September 1944 and it crashed near Elden, killing the pilot. It would appear that the wreckage was moved to the airfield at Deelen where, later, it was bulldozed into a bomb crater.

Chapter 15

Pocket Rocket

The Messerschmitt Me 163 was not a jet fighter but a rocket interceptor and, as such, it was the only rocket-powered aircraft to go operational in World War Two, but even then, there were only a few of them and not enough to have any impact on the air war.

Origins

The origins of what became known as the Komet go back to 1937 with the design of a delta-wing sailplane by Professor Alexander Lippisch. This resulted in the Deutsche Forschungsanstalt für Segelflug (DFS) 194 in 1938, which had a small propeller engine. However, in early 1939, Lippisch moved DFS to work with Messerschmitt, where the proposed aircraft would be fitted with a Walter HWK rocket motor, which was unique in that it used high-test peroxide (known as T-Stoff) as its propellant. In early 1941, the first prototypes began to be built, with initial test flying carried out without an engine. The first powered flight is believed to have taken place at the testing facility at Peenemünde in August 1941, and on 2 October 1941, the Me 163 set a new world air-speed record.

In December 1941, work began on redesigning the Me 163 as an operational interceptor that would be powered by the new Walter-Triebwerk RII-203 engine (which would be replaced by the HWK 109-509A-1 in 1943), which used hydrazine hydrate and methyl alcohol (known as C-Stoff) mixed with T-Stoff, a highly volatile mix that caused a number of problems, including the engine exploding or causing dreadful chemical burns to the pilot. The new airframe, designated the Me 163B, would be armed with either 20mm or 30mm cannon, which would now go to Erprobungskommando 16, the first Me 163s arriving for operational evaluation at Peenemünde in July 1943. However, following the RAF bombing in August 1943, the Me 163s moved to Bad Zwischenahn and then, in April 1944, I./JG 400 was formed at Wittmundhafen. Many pilots from Erprobungskommando 16 moved to this new unit, which received 13 Me 163s the following month.

Into combat

On 16 August 1944, a formation of B-17S encountered the Komet for the first time. The American crews were concerned that it was so fast they could not be tracked by turrets and waist guns; the German

Above left: **Me 163B-1 of I./JG 400 starts up.**

Above right: **General Adolf Galland (third from right) inspecting an Me 163 prototype.**

pilots Lt Hartmut Ryll and Fws Herbert 'Nicky' Straznicky and Siegfried Schübert of 1./JG 400 each claimed the destruction of a B-17 before P-51s of the 370th Fighter Sqn/ 359th Fighter Group intervened. Lt Col John Murphy claimed the destruction of one and helped 2/Lt Cyril Jones Jr in shooting down another. Ryll's Komet exploded over Bad Lausick, while Strasnicky fell victim to Sgt H Kaysen, a gunner from the 305th Bomb Group, but he managed to bale out near Böhlen.

Me 163B V18 broke the speed record on 6 July 1944.

Three more kills, two again to Siegfried Schübert and one to Lt Hans Bott, occurred in August 1944, with one more to Bott and Schubert in September 1944. Then there would be just two more claims until 3 March 1945 when Oblt August Hachtel claimed two more B-17s. So far, encounters with Komets had been an almost entirely American affair but this was about to change. On 7 March 1945, Flt Lt Ray Raby, flying a Spitfire of 542 Sqn on a reconnaissance sortie, was intercepted by two Komets. What happened was recorded in the 542 Sqn ORB: 'His targets were Bohlen, Moldis, Rosnitz, Chemnitz and Dresden. After covering Bohlen and Moldis, he was intercepted by two Me 163s when over Rositz. He took immediate evasive action and eventually evaded at 6,000ft. He then climbed up again to 20,000ft but was forced to abandon rest of sortie due to shortage of fuel.'

Nine days later would see a more conclusive combat. Oblt Rolf 'Bubi' Glogner of 2./JG 400, together with another unidentified pilot, took off shortly after dawn to intercept a Mosquito approaching Leipzig. This was an aircraft crewed by American Fg Off Raymond Hays and Flt Sgt Morgan Phillips of 544 Sqn. What then happened is best described by Raymond Hays' DFC citation:

This officer was the pilot of an aircraft detailed for a reconnaissance covering the Leipzig area in March 1945. Whilst over the target, two enemy fighters attempted to close in. Plt Off Hays took violent evading action. Much height was lost. At this stage another enemy aircraft joined the fight. Plt Off Hays maneuvered with great skill and although his aircraft was hit he succeeded in evading the attackers. The starboard engine had been badly damaged but course was set for home. Later on the return flight the aircraft was attacked by another fighter. Pilot Officer Hays maneuvered with superb skill. Although the aircraft sustained further damage and the navigator was wounded, this pilot succeeded in evading the fighter. He afterwards flew to a landing ground in Allied territory.

It would not be until April 1945 that the RAF recorded what it believed to be the first air combat success against the Komet, and that honour went to an Australian pilot. On 10 April 1945, 165 Sqn, flying Mustangs, recorded the following in its unofficial diary:

'10.4.45. Escort cover this day for 200 heavies to Leipzig. Another railway station was hit. An Me 163 (the little fat basket version of the jet) up from Halle shot down one bomber above the airfield and prepared to dive for a second attack on the formation.'

The target was a daylight attack on the Engelsdorf and Mockau railway yards by 134 Lancasters, 90 Halifaxes and six Mosquitos. The 165 Sqn diary wasn't exactly correct regarding the interception by this lone German fighter, the 405 Sqn ORB recording the following:

'In the target area, immediately following release of target indicators, Lancaster ME315/K was attacked by an Me 163. The attacking aircraft approached from the rear and above and with one burst completely shot away the rear turret, rudder and elevator. Damage was also caused to the H2S set and mid upper turret. The rear gunner, Flt Lt Mellstrom, was in his turret when the attack commenced and is believed killed.'

Signals monitoring later picked up a transmission to the effect that an Me 163 from I./JG 400 based at Brandis had shot down a Lancaster at 1802hrs, the exact same time that two bombers from 415 and 425 Sqns claimed to have damaged the rocket fighter, but these claims were later disallowed. It would appear the German pilot was Lt Fritz Kelb, who shortly afterwards transferred to fly Me 262s with 1./JG 7 where he shot down a B-17 Flying Fortress on 25 April 1945 only to be shot down himself and killed five days later. Oblt Rolf Glogner also claimed a Mosquito that day but this cannot be substantiated. However, despite what a number of the Lancaster gunners thought, they had not shot down the rocket fighter as 165 Sqn's diary shows:

'Fg Off Haslope chased him down, reached the calculated speed of 675mph in a dive from 25,000ft to 3,000ft. Firing all the time, he closed right in and actually overtook it achieving strikes all along the fuselage and wing roots. He claimed one damaged.'

Haslope's combat report shows that this combat was a dramatic event:

I noticed a bomber begin to smoke and something appeared to fly off it. This resolved itself into a Me 163 which climbed vertically at great speed. I reported the aircraft and dropped my overload tanks and gave chase at full throttle. The Me 163 turned towards me and I had a shot at him in a right hand turn, range about 900yds and 30 degrees deflection but observed no strikes. The Me 163 then spiralled into a vertical

Above left: Me 163A V4 first flew on 2 October 1941.

Above right: The difference between the Me 163A (right) and Me 163B-1.

dive which I followed, firing several bursts of about two to three seconds observing strikes on four occasions on the wing roots and several small pieces came off. I overshot rapidly at 3,000ft and had to pull up to avoid collision, wrinkling the wings as I did so. The Me 163 continued on down and was observed by Sqn Ldr Potocki of 315 Sqn and Fg Off Wacnik of 306 Sqn to hit the ground and explode at an airfield believed to be either Brandis or Mensdorf.

What they had probably seen explode was one of the two bombers lost in this attack – either a Halifax from 415 Sqn or a Lancaster from 433 Sqn.

There was one other RAF pilot who is credited with a Komet, albeit in unusual circumstances. On the evening of 14 April 1945, Sqn Ldr John Shepherd of 41 Sqn was leading three Spitfires on an armed reconnaissance in the Bremen area. As they approached Nordholz airfield, two unidentified aircraft were seen as Shepherd's combat report describes:

'Two aircraft were seen taking off. Diving on them I recognised them as an Me 163 being towed by an Me 110. I was closing very rapidly but managed to get in a short burst in on the Me 110 obtaining strikes on port engine and cockpit. The Me 110 went into a left-hand diving turn, turning over onto its back, and crashed into a field bursting into flames. The 163 appeared to break away from the 110 and make a wide left-hand turn, finally diving straight in about three fields away from the Me 110'.

Messerschmitt Bf 110s were used by JG 400 as tugs for Me 163 training flights and this one was flown by Ofw Werner Nelte. He had previously flown with Erprobungskommando 16 and had first flown the Me 163 in May 1944; in June 1944 he had to ditch in Lake Zwischenahn when the tug aircraft developed engine problems. He had then flown with I./JG 400 and it would appear he was now with II./JG 400, which was now moving from Nordholz to Husum. He was apparently in the process of towing an Me 163 to the new airfield when Shepherd attacked. Nelte was killed; the pilot of the Me 163 is not known but he survived the enforced landing.

End game

There would be just one more encounter between a Komet and the RAF when, on 22 April 1945, Oblt Franz Woidich of 6./JG 400 claimed an unidentified aircraft believed to have been a Lancaster, his 110th and last kill of the war. Seven hundred and sixty-seven aircraft attacked Bremen that day and although two Lancasters were lost and one was damaged, no mention was made of the presence of Komets.

The Komet was an incredible, if unorthodox, fighter. Difficult to handle, even by experienced pilots, most aircraft and pilots were lost in accidents as opposed to combat. Although the concept was good, it was another case of too little, too late for the Luftwaffe, which is why the RAF rarely encountered them in combat over Germany in 1945. With no fuel and Allied air superiority, most were found abandoned on German airfields at the end of the war, which is why today ten complete examples can be found in museums around the world.

Me 163B-1 of I./JG 400 about to get airborne.

Chapter 16
Heinkel's Nocturnal Hunter

The Heinkel He 219 had the potential to be the best night-fighter of the war. However, thanks to interference by senior officers, it never truly achieved the potential of which it was capable.

Need for change

In August 1940, Ernst Heinkel AG submitted outline designs for a revolutionary two-seat, twin-engine, high-speed heavy fighter that could also be used for bombing – the brainchild of designer Robert Lusser. Competition was stiff, notably against Messerschmitt's under-performing Me 210, which would then be superseded too late by the Me 410 and, as a result, the design did not immediately find favour. However, with an escalation of Bomber Command's attacks on Germany and a rapidly evolving Luftwaffe night-fighter force, in late 1941 Heinkel was tasked with further developing the design as a night-fighter and, in early 1942, detailed design began at Heinkel's Rostock-Marienehe factory in northern Germany. However, as a result of RAF bombing attacks on Rostock, production was hampered so much that design and development was moved to Vienna.

Despite the move, the first He 219 prototype flew at the start of November 1942, powered by two Daimler-Benz DB 603A engines (it should have been powered by the better DB 603G but, as usual with German aircraft engines, they were not available in time or in sufficient numbers). Unusually for German prototype aircraft, the results were good from the outset and in December 1942, the aircraft was flown to Peenemünde for weapons trials. Initially, two 20mm MG 151s were mounted in a pack under the fuselage with a 13mm MG 131 in the rear of the cockpit. The pack armament was soon changed to four 30mm MK 108s, while subsequent prototypes had six forward-firing 20mm MG 151s (four in the pack, two in the wing root). It was also fitted with FuG 202 Lichtenstein airborne interception radar. It was around then that the He 219 was unofficially named Uhu or Owl – quite an appropriate name for a nocturnal hunter.

He 219A fitted with FuG 220 Lichtenstein radar.

Into combat

The initial order for 100 He 219s placed in August 1942 was raised by another 200 in April 1943, and shortly afterwards, three examples of the prototypes were given to I./Nachtjagdgeschwader 1(I./NJG 1) for operational trials. I./NJG 1 was based at Venlo in Holland and was commanded by highly experienced night-fighter pilot Hptm Werner Streib.

Streib was initially a Bf 110 day fighter pilot with 2 Staffel/Zerstörergeschwader 1 (2./ZG 1) and got his first and only day kill on 10 May 1940. He was given command of 2 Staffel on 6 June 1940 but, shortly after, I./ZG 1 became I./NJG 1 and converted to night fighting. His first night kill was a Whitley of 51 Sqn on the night of 19 July 1940 and by 15 October 1940, he had shot down a total of nine aircraft (eight of them at night), had been promoted to Hauptmann and had been given command of I./NJG 1. His award for the Ritterkreuz in October 1940 came six days after he shot down three aircraft in one night. By the end of 1941, his score stood at 22, and by the end of 1942, it stood at 38. He would get his 40th kill on the night of 13 January 1943 and on 26 February 1943, he received the Eichenlaub to the Ritterkreuz. It was clear that he was the ideal pilot to prove the new night-fighter in combat, which he did spectacularly on the night of 11 June 1943.

Bomber Command's target that night was Düsseldorf and 43 RAF aircraft failed to return, with night-fighters claiming the destruction of 30. Five of these were claimed by Werner Streib flying the He 219 on its first operational sortie.

Streib, together with his equally experienced Bordfunker, Uffz Helmut Fischer, took off from Venlo at 0038hrs flying He 219V9 (the ninth prototype) Wk Nr 190009 coded G9+FB. The aircraft was controlled from the ground by the highly experienced fighter controller Oblt Walter Knickmeier who quickly directed Streib to his first victim – believed to be a Halifax of 408 Sqn flown by Plt Off Arthur Grant, which then crashed near Roermond at 0105hrs. Next was a Lancaster of 12 Sqn flown by Sgt Bob Highet, which he shot down near Rheinhberg at 0120hrs. At 0155hrs, he was directed onto a Halifax of 158 Sqn flown by Sgt Ron Pope, which he shot down at 0155hrs just outside Nijmegen. Kill number four came at 0216hrs south-west of Nijmegen and was believed to be a Lancaster of 115 Sqn flown by Sqn Ldr Doug Fox DFC. Six minutes later, he shot down a 78 Sqn Halifax flown by Flt Sgt Frank Hemmings at Sambeek. The He 219's first mission at the hands of Werner Streib had resulted in the deaths of 31 aircrew, with another four captured – an impressive first trial by combat .

However, the night did not go all Streib's way as, on landing at Venlo at 0302hrs, his Uhu suffered flap and cockpit instrument failures and he was forced to crash-land, the cockpit section breaking away. Both crew members suffered minor injuries and Fischer was admitted to hospital.

The pre-production He 219A-0 arrived on I./NJG 1 in August–September 1943 and would lose its first aircraft in combat on the night of 5 September 1943 when Ritterkreuz winner Oblt Heinz Strüning, Staffelkapitän of 3./NJG 1 was hit by return fire from his intended victim and with both engines hit, he and his Bordfunker Ofw Willi Bleier baled out of He 219A-0, Wk Nr 190010 G9+GL over Jülich. Strüning, whose score of victories stood at 40, was wounded, but Bleier hit the tail and was killed.

Above left: He 2129A-0 of Stab./NJG 1.

Above right: Hptm Werner Streib.

The first production variant to arrive on I./NJG 1 was the He 219A-2 (the A-1 was a reconnaissance version, which was abandoned). The A-2 was similar to the A-0 apart from improved DB 603A engines, which necessitated modified nacelles while internally it had additional fuel tanks. The A-3 (night-fighter), A-4 (high-altitude Mosquito hunter), A-5 (three-seat improved night-fighter) and A-6 (stripped-down Mosquito hunter) didn't really progress further than design or early prototype phases. The ultimate version would be the A-7, which had improved DB 603E engines and a normal armament of two 20mm MG151 cannon in the wing roots, two MG151/20s or MK108s in the gun pack and two 30mm MK108s behind the cockpit firing obliquely – the typical Schräge Musik installation for attacking bombers from underneath.

However, in spring 1944, Generalfeldmarschall Erhard Milch, who as Generalflugzeugmeister was in charge of aircraft production and had never really liked the He 219, ordered production of the He 219 to cease in favour of newer aircraft, most of which subsequently never made it into service. The He 219s currently on the production line at Rostock were finished in March 1945, development of subsequent variants such as the three-seat He 219B with the Junkers Jumo 222 engine never materialised. It would appear that the opportunity for the He 219 to make a difference had slipped away.

Eject eject

The Uhu was one of the first aircraft to be fitted with, and to use, combat ejection seats for its crew. The first successful use on operations came on the night of 11 April 1944 when Uffz Herter and Gefr Werner Perbix of 2./NJG 1 were attacked by an intruder near Weert in Holland. They were forced to eject at 2308hrs and both men survived. It is probable they were victims of a 239 Sqn Mosquito flown by Sqn Ldr Nevil Reeves, who reported shooting down a twin-tailed aircraft near Aachen believed to be this He 219. Nevil Reeves' report reads as follows:

> When seven miles north of Aachen the navigation lights of an aircraft flying west to east were seen some six to seven miles away at 15,000ft. Mosquito turned towards it losing height to 13,000ft but navigation lights were doused. Mosquito continued flying west and AI contact at 8,000ft was obtained but then lost to interference. Aircraft turned back towards Aachen climbing to 16,000ft and another AI contact obtained maximum range. Endeavouring to close in, a further head on contact at 14,000ft and a visual obtained of a Do 217. Aircraft fired at 150yds range and strikes were seen all over enemy aircraft which immediately

burst into flames. Mosquito peeled off to avoid collision. Enemy aircraft blazing fiercely was seen to hit the ground with a spectacular flash. Two parachutes were seen descending into clouds.

The shooting down of Lt Otto-Heinrich 'Heiner' Fries and his Bordfunker, Fw Alfred 'Fred' Staffa, of Stab II./NJG 1 at 0125hrs on 20 May 1944 in an He 219A-0 saw the next ejection. Wg Cdr Norman Starr of 605 Sqn was the only pilot to shoot down an unidentified aircraft that night, which was landing at Florennes airfield in Belgium. The He 219 crashed at S'Hertogenbosch in Holland, some distance away from Florennes. This crew, now flying with 2./NJG 1, would then be shot down by Flt Lt Ken Vaughan of 85 Sqn on the evening of 16 January 1945, and were again forced to eject, Otto Fries being badly injured this time. Fred Staffa then flew with Hptm Ernst-Wilhelm Modrow of 1./NJG 1 only to be shot down and forced to eject a third time on 1 February 1945. Only one claim for an He 219 that night was filed, by Flt Lt Jim Lomas of 25 Sqn near Bonn at around 2000hrs; this He 219 crashed at Siegburg at 1945hrs. Thus, Fred Staffa, who passed away in March 2014, had the honour of being one of the first, if not *the* first, to use an ejection seat and then did it twice more before the end of the war.

Mosquito hunter
Always an irritation to the Luftwaffe, Mosquitos didn't always have it their way, as the He 219 was regarded as being capable of shooting them down. At the end of January 1944, Nachtjagdgruppe 10 (NJGr 10) was formed at Werneuchen near Berlin, commanded by Maj Rudolf Schoenert, and was intended as an anti-Mosquito night-fighter unit. Formed with a mix of Fw 190s, Bf 109s, Bf 110s and Ju 88s, 3./NJGr 10, believed to have been commanded by Maj Harald Lange, did not receive its first He 219 until April 1944; its first kill then appears to have been by Oblt Friedrich Berger on 21 July 1944 but evidence now indicates that he was not flying an He 219. The first confirmed Mosquito kill by an He 219 was achieved by Oblt Werner Baake Staffelkapitän of 2./NJG 1 at 2335hrs on 6 May 1944. His victim was an aircraft from 109 Sqn, crewed by Sqn Ldr Harry Stephens DFC and Flt Lt Norman Fredman DFC, which was returning from a nuisance raid on Leverkusen. Their Mosquito crashed

Streib's He 219 after the crash on the night of 11 June 1943.

near Roermond in Holland, killing both crew members. Baake would go on to shoot down a total of 41 aircraft (but this was his one and only Mosquito), be awarded the Ritterkreuz and survive the war.

Around 340 He 219s were built, of which around 195 were delivered to operational units. It is therefore not surprising that many He 219s were captured at the end of the war. The RAE managed to obtain five airworthy examples, which were flown by such test pilots as Eric Brown. Brown commented that the cockpit was outstanding and that it was a good all-weather aircraft but concluded by saying:

> I would say that this Heinkel fighter's reputation was somewhat overrated. It was basically a good night-fighter in concept but suffered from what is perhaps the nastiest characteristic that any twin-engined aircraft can have – it was underpowered. Furthermore, it appeared to be short on performance to deal with the Mosquito, a task which was, in part, its raison d'etre but it was surely a very unpleasant handful for any four-engined bomber to encounter. One is led to wonder what changes might have taken place in the night skies of Germany had the Generalflugzeugmeister not been so resolutely opposed to this Heinkel creation or had the Heinkel organisation proven capable of delivering the He 219 in quantity.

He 219A, winter 1944–45.

Above left: He 219A of NJG 1 under attack by American fighters, 1945.

Above right: He 219 A-5/R2 formerly of 3./NJG 1 seen at RAE Farnborough after the war.

Chapter 17

Sparrow Goes to War

The Heinkel He 162 was intended to be a cheap and easy-to-make fighter but even though it made it to an operational unit, it was mostly found sitting and waiting for action when the war ended and it never had the chance to prove itself.

Emergency fighter
In the second week of September 1944, the RLM issued the requirement for an emergency lightweight fighter. It was to be powered by the BMW 003 turbojet – an engine not being used by the other jet-engined aircraft, namely the Me 262 and Arado 234. Of the eight companies approached to produce what was called a Völksjäger (literally 'People's Fighter'), Heinkel was the successful manufacturer with its He 162.

In addition to the engine, the RLM's specification called for the aircraft to be capable of 466mph (750kph) at sea-level, have a take-off run of 1,870ft (600m), be constructed from non-essential materials (namely wood) and could be mass produced at the optimistic rate of 1,000 per month. The RLM also specified what armament was to be carried and that it should be available by the start of January 1945. The He 162 was designed by Siegfried Günther and Karl Schwärzler, who had the initial designs complete by the start of November 1944, after which the prototypes would be built in Wien-Schwechat. However, due to Allied bombing, production would also be carried out at four other facilities, including one underground at Hinterbrühl near Wien. During the early phases, the construction programme was codenamed Salamander, the prototype construction site at Hinterbrühl was codenamed Languste (Crayfish) but Heinkel unofficially nicknamed the He 162 Spatz (Sparrow).

Amazingly, the first prototype got airborne on 6 December 1944, just 90 days after the specification was issued. However, if things had been smooth until now, problems soon arose. As Heinkel's chief test pilot, Flugkapitän Gotthold Peter, got airborne, an undercarriage door broke away, apparently due to the

He 162M6 about to get airborne on 23 January 1945.

wooden door being inadequately glued. He also reported that the aircraft tended to pull to the left, but the engine performed well and the aircraft climbed to just under 20,000ft (6,000m) and achieved a speed of 522mph (840kph). Buoyed by what was deemed a success, on 10 December 1944, Gotthold Peter demonstrated the aircraft to senior Luftwaffe officers and high-ranking Nazi party officials at Schwechat. After what was a successful display, Peter decided to finish with a low-level high-speed pass over the airfield, during which the starboard wing leading edge broke away, the upper skinning began to roll back, the aircraft went into a roll, the aileron broke off and the aircraft hit the ground just outside the airfield boundary, killing Peter. Heinkel again blamed the glue – apparently the manufacturer's factory had been bombed, resulting in them having to use a sub-standard alternative.

Despite the crash of the first prototype, wings were ordered to be strengthened, and speed and full control limitations were imposed. Due to the instability of the aircraft around the vertical and horizontal axes, aerodynamicist Alexander Lippisch proposed wing-tip extensions, which became known as Lippisch Ears. These added to bringing the aircraft's centre of gravity further forward, and changes to the tail meant the initial problems experienced by the first prototype were apparently sorted. Furthermore, two 30mm MK108 cannon, fitted to the first prototype, were now standard fits, with two lighter 20mm MG151s being fitted to the seventh and subsequent prototypes.

Despite this, problems still arose. In January 1945, the third and fourth prototypes were damaged in accidents and then, on 4 February 1945, Georg Weydemeyer, another experienced pilot, was killed when the sixth prototype's rudder jammed and the aircraft crashed. Then Flugbaumeister Full was killed when the third prototype crashed on 25 February 1945, the cause yet again stated as being instability and a possible engine fire.

Nevertheless, development continued as best it could and it soon resulted in the pre-production version, the He 162A-0. This was quickly followed by the A-1, which had two 30mm guns and minor internal differences to the A-2, which had two 20mm guns. The Sparrow was *almost* ready to fight.

He 162M1 first flew on 6 December 1944 only to crash four days later.

Operational

Operational testing of the He 162 was given to Erprobungskommando 162 at Rechlin, commanded by the highly experienced and decorated fighter pilot Oberstleutnant Heinz Bär. Formed in January 1945, most of the initial flying was led by another experienced fighter pilot, Hptm Horst Geyer, Bär and Geyer having flown Bf 109s with Jagdgeschwader 51 (JG 51) in the Battle of Britain and Geyer having been involved with the Me 262 development. It soon became obvious that any intention for less experienced pilots, glider pilots or suitably qualified Hitler Youth pilots to fly this 'simple' aircraft was flawed and the intended formation of the He 162-equipped I./JG 80 at Goslar was cancelled. Instead, it was decided to withdraw I and II Gruppe/JG 1 from the front line and to convert the pilots from the Fw 190A-8 to the He 162A-2.

JG 1 was commanded by Oberstleutnant Herbert Ihlefeld, another experienced fighter pilot who had also flown in the Battle of Britain. However, having been wounded in action on 1 January 1945, it is believed he left the flying to Maj Werner Zober's I./JG 1 and Hptm Paul-Heinrich Dähne's II./JG 1. On 30 January 1945, the order for these two Gruppes to convert to the He 162 was given and they headed for Parchim where training would start. However, due to the chaotic state of Germany at the time, the first pilots from I./JG 1 did not arrive at Schwechat, Marienehe or Bernburg (sites where the He 162s were being assembled and therefore a source of aircraft) until the end of February 1945. Meanwhile, training for groundcrew was taking place at Parchim –not the best situation for a cohesive fighter unit.

It was not long before the first accidents occurred. At Schwechat on 12 March 1945, Feldwebel Wanke's eighth prototype suffered engine failure, crashed and caught fire, Feldwebel Gerhard Gleuwitz suffered an accident in prototype 26 while Uffz Siegfried Tautz crashed on landing the nineteenth prototype, hitting some oil drums; the aircraft turned over and caught fire, killing Tautz. All three pilots were apparently from Hptm Wolfgang Ludewig's 2./JG 1.

With minimum training, on 31 March 1945, I./JG 1 returned to Parchim, while II./JG 1 moved to Rostock to convert to the He 162 at the Heinkel factory. Eventually, I./JG 1 arrived at Leck in Schleswig-Holstein on 16 April 1945, but with three weeks of the war left, any impact the Sparrow could make would be minimal.

The only combat loss

Records at this late stage of the war are imprecise but up to 19 April 1945, all the He 162 losses had been as a result of accidents. This would change at midday on that day. Late that morning, eight Hawker Tempests of 222 Sqn, led by Flt Lt Harry Turney, got airborne in excellent flying weather for a fighter sweep of the airfields at Neumünster, Schleswig and Husum. At Schleswig, they damaged a total of eight He 111s, Ju 87s and Ju 88s, while Flt Lt Vic Berg destroyed a Ju 88. However, at what he stated was Husum, Fg Off Geoff Walkington saw something different as his combat report states:

> I was flying as Blue 1 strafing Husum airfield when I sighted an aircraft flying in a northerly direction away from the aerodrome. I immediately broke off my attack on the airfield and chased this aircraft which

was camouflaged mottled green with a yellow underside and appeared to have twin fins and rudders and one engine. The nose of the aircraft had a drooping appearance and the wings (plan view) resembled those of an Me 109. Due to my loss of speed on turning the enemy aircraft pulled away to about 1,500yds. Having recognised this aircraft as hostile by its camouflage, I gave chase, but was unable to close, my IAS being 360mph. The enemy aircraft did a 360 degrees turn to starboard which I followed, turning inside. During my turn I managed to close to 1,000yds. Being unable to gain further I trimmed my aircraft carefully and allowing about three quarters of a ring above enemy aircraft I fired short bursts. Enemy aircraft then pulled up through cloud which was 8/10ths at 3,000ft; I followed through a gap and passed enemy aircraft spinning down out of control from approx. 3,500ft. I then watched enemy aircraft explode on the ground near Husum aerodrome.

Walkington reported his combat as taking place at 1220hrs. At 1222hrs, a pair of He 162s from Oblt Emil Demuth's 3./JG 1, flown by Lt Gerhard Stiemer and Feldwebel Günther Kirchner, scrambled from Leck to intercept enemy fighters reported in the vicinity. Having only just got airborne, they were attacked by what they thought were P-47 Thunderbolts. Stiemer looked behind to see the canopy of Kirchner's aircraft blow away and the pilot's ejection seat shoot into the air:

'We had hardly reached an altitude of 50m, when we were attacked from the rear. Though Kirchner succeeded in ejecting his seat, the lack of altitude was not sufficient to allow his parachute to open and my comrade fell to his death. I was much luckier and managed to escape, but then I could not lower my undercarriage! I approached the airfield flying at the lowest altitude and landed as quickly as I could.'

This was the first known incident of a pilot deploying the catapult seat installed in the He 162, the ejection seat having been perfected by Heinkel who also used it on the He 219. The parachute was stored in the seat pan and it was cartridge as opposed to compressed-air fired.

Kirchner crashed at Klintum, just south of Leck, which does not match with Walkington's location of Husum, which is further south. However, there were no other recorded claims that day in that approximate area and at that time. Furthermore, Walkington's description of what he attacked appears to match with what would appear to be an He 162.

He 162A-2 of I./JG 1 captured at Leck at the end of the war.

The sight that greeted the Allies at Leck, May 1945.

Not enough time

In the days that followed, Lt Rudi Schmitt of Hptm Heinz Künnecke's 1./JG 1 ejected near Leck, while Feldwebel Erwin Steeb of Oblt Zipprecht's 6./JG 1 became the first II./JG 1 pilot to bale out, II Gruppe still in training on the type although whether he ejected or not is unknown. The next casualty would be Gruppen Kommandeur Hptm Paul-Heinrich Dähne, a Knight Cross holder with 99 kills. On a training flight, he encountered problems and tried to eject but the canopy failed to detach and he was killed.

Some records also state that before his death on 19 April 1945, Feldwebel Günther Kirchner had shot down a Tempest whose pilot was captured, but this cannot be substantiated. Similarly, Uffz Helmut Reichenbach of 2./JG 1 apparently shot down an aircraft on 26 April 1945, after which he crashed in unknown circumstances and was killed, but again nothing matches. Then, on 4 May 1945, Lt Rudolf Schmidt of 1./JG 1 claimed a Typhoon; again, nothing matches.

On 2 May 1945, II./JG 1 arrived at Leck. Two days later, due to a shortage of aircraft, pilots and logistical support, I./JG 1 was restructured to be 1 (Einsatz) Staffel, commanded by Maj Werner Zober, and 2 (Einsatz) Staffel, commanded by Hptm Wolfgang Ludewig. Four days later, Germany surrendered, and when British troops arrived at Leck, they found JG 1's pristine He 162s lined up, ready for action; proof of what could have been but never happened.

The RAF had at least 11 airworthy He 162s to choose from but the lack of documentation or pilots' notes made it a daunting prospect to get into one, start it up, take off and land, but that is exactly what test pilot Capt Eric 'Winkle' Brown did on 7 September 1945. He later wrote of the He 162:

'It would have certainly have been an effective gun platform and its small dimensions would have rendered it difficult to hit. Even if somewhat underpowered, it had good performance-it could certainly have run rungs around the contemporary Meteor. However, it was no aeroplane to let embryo pilots loose on and it would have demanded more than simply a good pilot to operate it out of a small airfield'.

Despite the plethora of He 162s captured at Leck and in factories, most were scrapped after evaluation but seven complete examples still exist in the world; all but one are A-2 variants. The RAF Museum in Hendon and the Imperial War Museum in London each have one, and both wear JG 1's markings.

A pilot of I./JG 1 alongside his He 219A-2, Leck, May 1945.

An He 162 being evaluated by the French Air Force, 1946.

Chapter 18
Red Hearts Over Malta

The first German single-engined fighter to make an appearance over Malta did not do so until 12 February 1941 and made an immediate impact by shooting down three Hurricanes. Between then and 25 May 1941, 7 Staffel/Jagdgeschwader 26 (7./JG 26), whose aircraft sported a red or sometimes black heart on the cowlings of its Messerschmitt Bf 109s, accounted for 48 RAF aircraft – both on the air and on the ground – 20 of these being flown by former Battle of Britain pilots; during this time, they suffered not a single loss.

Battle of Britain

7./JG 26, commanded by Oblt Georg Beyer, had experienced a hard Battle of Britain. Based at Caffiers and Abbeville-Drucat, it began operations over Britain on 21 July 1940 and three days later scored its first victory. The following day saw claims for four more Spitfires and, from 14 August 1940, claims would increase but, at the same time, so would losses. By 14 November 1940, the Staffel had claimed 31 RAF aircraft and by the end of 1940, it had suffered five pilots killed or missing and eight captured.

However, as a result of changes in the command of fighter units, which saw Maj Adolf Galland moving from III Gruppe./JG 26 to be Geschwader Kommodore of JG 26, a new name emerged in 7./JG 26. When Galland moved, he took Oblt Georg Beyer with him as his adjutant (Beyer would last just seven days before he was shot down and taken prisoner on 28 August 1940). Beyer's place was taken by 22-year-old Oblt Joachim 'Jochen' Müncheberg, who had become adjutant of III./JG 26 on 23 September 1939. His first kill was a Bristol Blenheim of 57 Sqn flown by Plt Off Harry Bewlay on 7 November 1939 and, by the time he came to 7 Staffel, he had shot down 13 aircraft. His first kill with his new Staffel was a Hurricane on 24 August 1940 and by 14 September 1940, he had achieved 20 kills, which resulted in the award of the Ritterkreuz. He would shoot down just three more aircraft in 1940, the last being a Spitfire off Dover on 14 November 1940, and he would have to wait just under another three months to increase his score.

By the end of 1940, it was clear to the Germans that Malta was a threat to their operations in the Mediterranean, and in December 1940, X. Fliegerkorps relocated from Norway to Taormina on the east coast of Sicily, with various combat units following afterwards. The first German attack on Malta occurred

Above left: Jochen Müncheberg celebrating a victory.

Above right: Technical work being carried out on a Bf 109E-3 of 7./JG 26.

Believed to have been taken at Gela, in early 1941. A Bf 109E-7 of 7./JG 26 can be seen in the foreground, while in the background is a Bf 110 of 9./ZG 26. (via the late Dr A Price)

on 10 January 1941, after which, air attacks became an almost daily occurrence. The only RAF fighter squadron on the island was the Hurricane-equipped 261 Sqn, which was more than capable of countering the only German fighter unit, the Bf 110-equipped III./Zerstörergeschwader 26. However, with the Italians struggling in Libya, the Bf 110s moved to North Africa and were replaced by 7./JG 26.

Groundcrew had left Belgium on or around 22 January 1941 and met up with their pilots in Rome. They had returned to Germany to re-equip with the Bf 109E-7, an E-4 version capable of carrying a long-range tank that would give greater range and an ability to loiter over Malta – luxuries the Germans never had in the Battle of Britain. So it was, that on or around 9 February 1941, 7./JG 26 arrived at Gela on the southern coast of Sicily and, three days later, flew its first mission over Malta.

The battle begins

On the afternoon of 12 February 1941, the Staffel, led by Müncheberg, was tasked to escort a reconnaissance mission, after which it would carry out a Freie Jagd (fighter sweep) over the island. As expected, 261 Sqn was scrambled only to be bounced by the Red Hearts, the first kill going to Müncheberg and another two to Ofw Werner Liebing. Flt Lt Gerald Watson was shot down into the sea and killed, his body never being recovered. Plt Off David Thacker, who had flown Hurricanes with 32 Sqn in the Battle of Britain and had only been in Malta for two weeks, was shot down over St Paul's Bay and baled out wounded, while Flt Lt Harry Bradbury crash-landed at Hal Far, suffering wounds. It is thought that one RAF pilot claimed to have shot down a Bf 109; not even one was damaged.

Conscious there were Bf 109s operating over Malta, the following day, aircraft from 261 Sqn climbed to 22,000ft and waited to pounce on four Bf 109s. However, they were spotted and the German fighters sped away. Two days later, things were different. On the morning of 16 February, two Schwarm of four aircraft, each led by Müncheberg and Oblt Klaus Mietusch, escorted Stukas attacking the airfield at Luqa. The RAF's response came from eight 261 Sqn Hurricanes, led by Flt Lt James MacLachlan DFC. MacLachlan was an experienced pre-war pilot having converted to Hurricanes from Fairy Battles after the Battle of France. He then flew with 73 and 145 Sqns in the Battle of Britain and arrived in Malta in November 1940. He had already claimed a total of seven Italian and German aircraft destroyed and one probable, but that day his luck ran out. The Hurricanes were bounced by Müncheberg, who accounted for MacLachlan – he baled out, badly wounded, and his left arm had to be amputated. The bounce then forced the remaining Hurricanes to fly towards Mietusch's Schwarm, which scattered them further, with the Germans claiming another two Hurricanes. However, Plt Off Allan McAdam and Fg Off Spencer 'Teddy' Peacock-Edwards both landed with damaged aircraft.

With 261 Sqn doing badly, it was a relief that the next Bf 109 appearance was not until 24 February 1941, but both sides came away empty handed. The following day, Müncheberg shot down Canadian Plt Off John Walsh. Walsh had flown with 615 Sqn in the Battle of Britain and had arrived in Malta at the end of January 1941. He had been credited with a Dornier 215 damaged earlier that day, only to apparently suffer engine problems that afternoon and was easily picked off by Müncheberg. Walsh baled out over St Paul's Bay and was rescued from the sea, suffering a leg broken in four places and a broken arm; he died of shock and pneumonia on 2 March 1941.

Right: **Klaus Mietusch (second from right). To his left is Oblt Heinz Ebeling (9./JG 26), and to his right is Oblt Gustav 'Micky' Sprick (8./JG 26). Sprick was awarded the Ritterkreuz on 1 October 1940 († 28 June 1941); Mietusch was awarded the Oakleaves for the Ritterkreuz after his death on 17 September 1944, while Ebeling was awarded the Ritterkreuz on 5 November 1940 – the very day he was captured.**

Below: **Sgt Bert Deacon's Hurricane after meeting with 7./JG 26, 11 April 1941. (via Thomas)**

Getting worse

If 261 Sqn had suffered badly so far, the following day would be even worse. With the Luftwaffe carrying out its heaviest air attack yet, 261 Sqn managed a single victory but sustained heavy losses at the hands of 7 Staffel and Italian fighters. In the space of 17 minutes, Müncheberg claimed two Hurricanes, while Oblt Klaus Mietusch and Uffz Georg Mondry claimed one more each. 261 Sqn's incomplete records mention five Hurricanes lost that day but the only pilots that can be linked to these losses were Plt Offs Phil Kearsey, Charles Langdon and Fred 'Eric' Taylor. Kearsey and Langdon were both ex-Battle of Britain pilots, while Eric Taylor was the top-scoring RAF pilot in Malta to date. He had arrived in Malta in June 1940 and became a founding member of the Hal Far Fighter Flight. He shot down his first aircraft on 10 July 1940 and by 26 February 1941 had been credited with seven destroyed, one probable and one damaged. He was last seen chasing a Stuka for which he was credited with its probable destruction, but he was also seen to be chased by a Bf 109. All three RAF pilots were reported missing and, again, all German aircraft returned unscathed.

Thankfully for the depleted 261 Sqn, there was now a break and the Red Hearts did not put in an appearance again until 2 March 1941 when, at 1045hrs, 2km west of Marsa Sciocco, Müncheberg, leading just two Bf 109s, bounced what they thought were Hurricanes, Müncheberg claiming to have shot down one. This was in fact a Fairey Fulmar of 806 Sqn flown by Lt Bill Barnes, which was being used as an emergency fighter. Barnes was an ace by this time, having been credited with six plus two shared destroyed and six plus two shared damaged between 2 September 1940 and 16 January 1941. Barnes had also flown Skuas with 806 Sqn over Norway and Dunkirk. He managed to land safely with a damaged aircraft but, later that day, he was a passenger in a car that failed to stop when challenged and he was accidentally killed by a sentry.

The result of 7./JG 26's strafing of Fg Off Len Rees' Sunderland, 27 April 1941. (via Thomas)

5 March 1941 would see a change when I./JG 27, which was transiting through Gela on its way to North Africa, accompanied 7./JG 26 with Müncheberg and an unknown pilot claiming a Hurricane each and Lt Willi Kothmann of 2./JG 27 claiming one. Two Hurricanes from 261 Sqn were lost – Sgt Harry Ayre managed to crash-land but immediately took off again to claim a Ju 88 destroyed and a third share in a Do 17 (but was probably a Bf 110), while Sgt Charles MacDougal, who had flown with 111 Sqn in the Battle of Britain, was shot down and killed just after claiming to have shot down a Ju 87. To add insult to injury, the Bf 109s then strafed aircraft and ships in St Paul's Bay, a clear sign of the air superiority they had achieved and a tactic that paid dividends two days later.

At midday on 7 March 1941, two pairs of Bf 109s chased and shot down a 69 Sqn Maryland returning from a reconnaissance of Taormina. Pilot Fg Off John Boys-Stones and one of his crew were killed, their aircraft crashing at Wied Tal Kleigha, while an escorting Hurricane from 261 Sqn was shot down into the sea; the pilot,

Sgt Ernest Jessop, was uninjured. They then strafed a moored 228 Sqn Sunderland in St Paul's Bay, badly damaging it and killing a guard; the Sunderland would be destroyed in another strafing attack by 7./JG 26 three days later.

The next RAF casualty did not occur until breakfast time on 15 March 1941. Three Wellingtons of 3 Gp Training Flt had flown from RAF Stradishall to Gibraltar and then took off at dawn for Malta. Unfortunately, one of them, flown by Sgt John Crawford and Sgt Richard Alington, was intercepted by Müncheberg north-west of Gozo; the crew of six plus a passenger (Gp Capt Dudley Humphreys) were all killed. Then, on 17 March 1941, 261 Sqn at last received reinforcements in the form of six 274 Sqn Hurricanes led by ace Fg Off Ernest 'Imshi' Mason DFC. However, on the afternoon of 22 March 1941, eight Hurricanes of 261 Sqn chased German bombers back towards Sicily. When they were about 20–40 km north of Malta, they were bounced by 7./JG 26, which claimed seven aircraft shot down. Fg Off James Foxton (a pilot from 69 Sqn), Sgt Dick Spyer, Plt Off Tom Garland, Fg Off John Southwell and Plt Off Dennis Knight were all shot down and reported missing. Despite 261 Sqn submitting claims for at least two Bf 109s, none was damaged.

There would be two more casualties before March 1941 was over. The month saw Müncheberg flying his 200th operational flight and shooting down his 33rd aircraft, again from 261 Sqn, on 28 March. Sgt Reg Goode was seriously wounded in the back and neck, but despite his Hurricane being badly damaged, he managed to crash-land at Ghain Tuffieha. Sgt Alex Livingston's Hurricane was also damaged in the same combat, but he successfully landed at Luqa.

Brief respite

Between 3 and 10 April 1941, there were no Bf 109 sightings as, for much of this period, 7./JG 26 was operating from Taranto on mainland Italy in support of the German invasion of Yugoslavia and Greece. This was fortuitous for the RAF since, on the morning of 2 April 1941, ten Hurricanes and two Skuas arrived from Gibraltar; the following day saw the arrival of 12 Hurricane IIs and nine Fulmar fighters of 800 Sqn.

On 11 April 1941, eight Hurricanes were scrambled only to be bounced, which resulted in two of the recently arrived pilots, Plt Off Peter Kennett and Sgt Peter Waghorn, being shot down into the sea and killed. Furthermore, three more Hurricanes crash-landed due to combat damage, their pilots being uninjured. The victors in this case were Müncheberg (two) and Klaus Mietusch and it was the latter who scored the next victory. Late morning on 13 April 1941, Fg Off 'Imshi' Mason claimed a Bf 109 just off the island only to be attacked by Mietusch. Mason succeeded in levelling out just above the sea but then his engine failed. He was quickly rescued from the sea and rushed to hospital where he was found to have bullet wounds to his right arm and left elbow, metal splinters in his left leg and skull as well as facial injuries, which included a broken nose from being thrown against the gun sight. Again, another Hurricane returned damaged and no Bf 109s were lost.

On 21 April 1941, each side claimed kills but no aircraft were lost. However, the next combat on, 23 April 1941, had a sad outcome when Jochen Müncheberg shot down Fg Off Henri Auger of 261 Sqn into the sea off Delimara. He was seen to bale out and land between Filfa and the mainland, but as there were still German aircraft around, no rescue launch was sent out and Auger is still listed as missing.

7./JG 26 would prowl over the island for just another month but during that time, it would claim another 17 aircraft in the air and on the sea and ground, starting with a Sunderland of 228 Sqn at Kalafrana on 27 April 1941. This date saw the arrival of 23 Hurricanes (which formed 185 Sqn) some of which were led in by Plt Off Leonard Rees' Sunderland but, as it landed, two Bf 109s strafed it, setting it on fire. Two days later, two Hurricanes were claimed as well as one the day after but these cannot be substantiated.

Oblt Erbo Graf von Kageneck, 9./JG 27.

As well as pure fighter missions, III./JG 27 also acted as fighter bombers.

On 1 May 1941 Jochen Müncheberg claimed three kills, which took him to 41 in total and resulted in the award of the Oak Leaves for the Ritterkreuz four days later. The Germans claimed five Hurricanes in two sorties that day, the only recorded losses being ex-Battle of Britain pilot Plt Off Bob Innes who baled out, his Hurricane crashing at Ghaxaq, and Sgt Brian Walmsley, who was wounded on the second sortie. For the first flight, records state one Hurricane was damaged and another shot down, the pilot was safe but there are no further details. 6 May 1941 would see another two victories for Müncheberg, who was joined by Oblt Erbo Graf von Kageneck of 9./JG 27, III./JG 27 having recently arrived at Gela on its way to North Africa. Plt Offs Alan Dredge, Colin Gray and Peter Thompson (all ex-Battle of Britain pilots) and Sgt Richard Branson were all wounded, with Gray and Branson baling out.

On 10 May 1941, another Sunderland from 10 Sqn Royal Australian Air Force (RAAF) was set on fire at Marsaxlokk Bay, strafed by a lone Bf 109 of 7./JG 26. Three days later saw the last victory over Malta for the Staffel when Klaus Mietusch (together with Erbo Graf von Kageneck) accounted for Flt Lt Innes Westmacott, who baled out wounded, and Plt Off Peter Thompson, who was killed. Three more kills would be credited to III./JG 27 on 14, 15 and 20 May (two from 261 Sqn and one from 185 Sqn) before, on 25 May 1941, 7./JG 26 made a spectacular last show before its departure for Greece and North Africa as the Ta Qali diary relates:

'Me 109s machine-gunned a searchlight station on the airfield, wounding one gunner. Two Hurricanes are burned out and three others seriously damaged on the ground (but repairable). A Lister engine is damaged and 90 gallons of oil are lost. One pilot and one airman are injured by shrapnel and admitted to hospital; two other airmen are slightly wounded'.

It was a baptism of fire for the recently arrived 249 Sqn.

In its short time over Malta, 7./JG 26, under the leadership of Jochen Müncheberg, had done extremely well compared to the Battle of Britain but its success would not be repeated in the months and years that followed. Many of the pilots that flew over Malta during those three months, including Müncheberg, would not survive the war.

Chapter 19
Night-Fighter Ace

The Bf 110 proved itself to be a potent night-fighter, with many German aces achieving the majority of their kills on this type. The career of Helmut Bergmann is very typical of many German night-fighter pilots who fought and subsequently died in the night skies over Europe during the last war.

Into action

Helmut Bergmann was born in Bochum in the Ruhr region of Germany. After initial training, he found himself posted to the Ergänzungstaffel/Nachtjagdgeschwader 1 on 15 July 1941, before being posted to 7 Staffel/NJG 4 (7/NJG 4) in the beginning of May 1942. At that time, NJG 4 was based at Juvincourt in north-east France and was ideally located for intercepting RAF bombers headed for or returning from Germany.

Bergmann had to wait until just past midnight on 20 September 1942 to get his first kill of the war, which was recorded as being a Whitley that crashed 10km south of the World War Two battlefield at Verdun. The German pilot's aircraft identification was not perfect as no Whitleys were operating over that part of Europe that night – his victim was probably a 35 Sqn Halifax flown by the commanding officer, Wg Cdr 'Jimmy' Marks DSO and Bar, DFC and Bar, whose flight engineer clearly recalls the attack:

'The Skipper immediately took the necessary action to leave the target area and we climbed away. As we did so, I saw an Me 110 flash past our starboard wing tip, nearly colliding with us. We levelled out at 11,000ft and passed out of Germany into France. I was calculating the fuel consumption and our reserves when there was a tremendous explosion in our port wing. I stood up and looked out – it appeared that numbers 5 and 6 fuel tanks were on fire, the flames going back and beyond the rear turret'.

This was destined to be Bergmann's first of 37 kills in two years, but his most spectacular feat occurred in the early hours of 11 April 1944. By this time, the 23-year-old had shot down 18 RAF bombers as well as being shot down himself twice (baling out once) and having to bale out during one mission due to engine failure.

Oblt Helmut Bergmann.

Spectacular night

Just after 0200hrs on the night of Easter Monday 1944, he lifted his fighter off from Juvincourt and headed north-east. He was immediately directed onto the RAF bomber stream, which was headed for the railway yards at Aulnoye. The attack on Aulnoye was regarded by Bomber Command as a 'milk run' due to its predicted ease and lack of risk. However, for seven of the attacking force, Bergmann was to prove this wrong.

Just eight minutes after getting airborne, he spotted an aircraft:

Bf 110D night-fighter, which was similar to what Bergmann flew initially.

'Near the ground were several green cascades which marked the RAF objective. Over the target, I fired at what I now identify as being a Lancaster from below and 100m range. He crashed immediately, his wings and fuselage ablaze, just north of the target at 0220hrs'.

His victim was from 460 Sqn; Fg Off Arthur Probert and his crew of six were all killed. Now firmly lodged in the bomber stream, Helmut could see Lancasters all around him, all of which suddenly veered away after seeing the fate of the 460 Sqn bomber. Nevertheless, ten minutes later he closed in on another Lancaster, this time from 576 Sqn and flown by Flt Lt Frank Barnsdale. Two minutes later, the Lancaster exploded on hitting the ground, killing all seven crew.

Two more victories quickly followed. There was just one survivor from the 12 Sqn Lancaster captained by Plt Off Frank Richards and, yet again, there were no survivors from the experienced crew of Flt Lt Richard Picton DFC of 550 Sqn. So far, Bergmann had caused the deaths of 27 airmen and his night was still not over, even if his next two victims were a little luckier than the previous four:

'I recognised the 5th and 6th enemy planes flying south-east within a searchlight area. I attacked the first one from below and fired from a distance of 80m into the starboard wing, immediately causing a fire. The burning plane was caught by searchlights and kept illuminated until the crash at 0250hrs at Beauquesne'.

The attack was a total surprise to the crew of a 103 Sqn Lancaster flown by Plt Off John Armstrong, whose wireless operator recalls:

I heard a loud bang and turned in my seat and saw flames behind me. For some inexplicable reason, I grabbed a fire extinguisher but soon realised it was a useless effort. I tried to call the Skipper but the intercom had been rendered useless. I looked forward and saw that the navigator and the engineer had gone. I went forward, after grabbing my 'chute, and putting it on, and saw the pilot trying to keep the aircraft steady, and continued to the escape hatch and jumped. I realised my luck when by the time the 'chute had opened, the Lancaster was already burning on the ground.'

Immediately after shooting down victim number five, Bergmann saw another target, a 101 Sqn Lancaster flown by Flt Lt Neil Nimmo:

'I spotted the Lancaster a few minutes later. She seemed to try and evade the searchlights. I opened fire at 0252hrs from a distance of 100m from below into the fuselage and into the right wing. Fire started at once with a bright flame. The burning plane was again kept in the searchlights and at 0254hrs I noticed burning wreckage on the ground'.

Four survived from each of the hit aircraft (victims five and six) but, sadly, three also died in each crash.

Short on fuel, Bergmann now turned eastwards and back towards Juvincourt but not before accounting for Plt Off Bill Green's 625 Sqn's Lancaster; another six crew were killed and one was taken prisoner.

Helmut Bergmann celebrated his 24th birthday just a month later, a late birthday present being the Ritterkreuz, which was awarded on 9 June 1944 and went with his Deutches Kreuz in Gold, awarded 6 March 1944. In the two months that followed his extraordinary feat of seven kills in one action, he shot down a further nine RAF bombers, six of these being on 4 May 1944 in circumstances similar to what happened on 11 April 1944.

Out of luck

However, the night skies over Europe were becoming a dangerous place for German night-fighters, no matter how experienced they were. Air superiority by day was also being achieved by night, especially by RAF Mosquitos and it was one of these that would become Bergmann's nemesis.

Wg Cdr Jimmy Marks, 35 Sqn, Bergmann's first victory.

Just after midnight on 7 July 1944, Flt Lt John Surman of 604 Sqn took off to carry out a defensive patrol over the Cherbourg Peninsula. At the same time, Bergmann and another Bf 110 took off to carry out ground attacks against Allied troop concentrations and vehicles. While orbiting, looking for targets, Bergmann was detected by both Allied ground radar and John Surman, as the latter recalls:

'I identified the target as a Messerschmitt 110. I closed in to 600ft, gave a two second burst and saw an explosion in the port engine and fuselage and starboard engine. The enemy aircraft dropped out of the sky and exploded on hitting the ground'.

So died Helmut Bergmann. His remains were initially buried as an unknown German airman but later he and his crew were exhumed and identified, and they now lie in the German Military Cemetery at Marigny, close to the town of St Lo. Bergmann's feat of shooting down seven aircraft in 46 minutes was only bettered by three other German night-fighter pilots and equalled by another four, little consolation for the 38 Allied aircrew who lost their lives on the night of Easter Monday 1944.

Above left: Victory 5: A 7 Sqn Stirling shot down near Charleville, 9 March 1943.

Above right: Victory 6: A 35 Sqn Halifax shot down near Sedan, 11 April 1943.

Above and right: Victory 7: A 425 Sqn Wellington shot down near Dallon, 15 April 1943. The 425 Sqn code and aircraft serial are clearly visible in the second photograph.

Above left: Bergmann has revisited his ninth victory by air – another 35 Sqn Halifax on 16 April 1943.

Above right: Victory 14: A 50 Sqn Lancaster near Almelo, 13 June 1943.

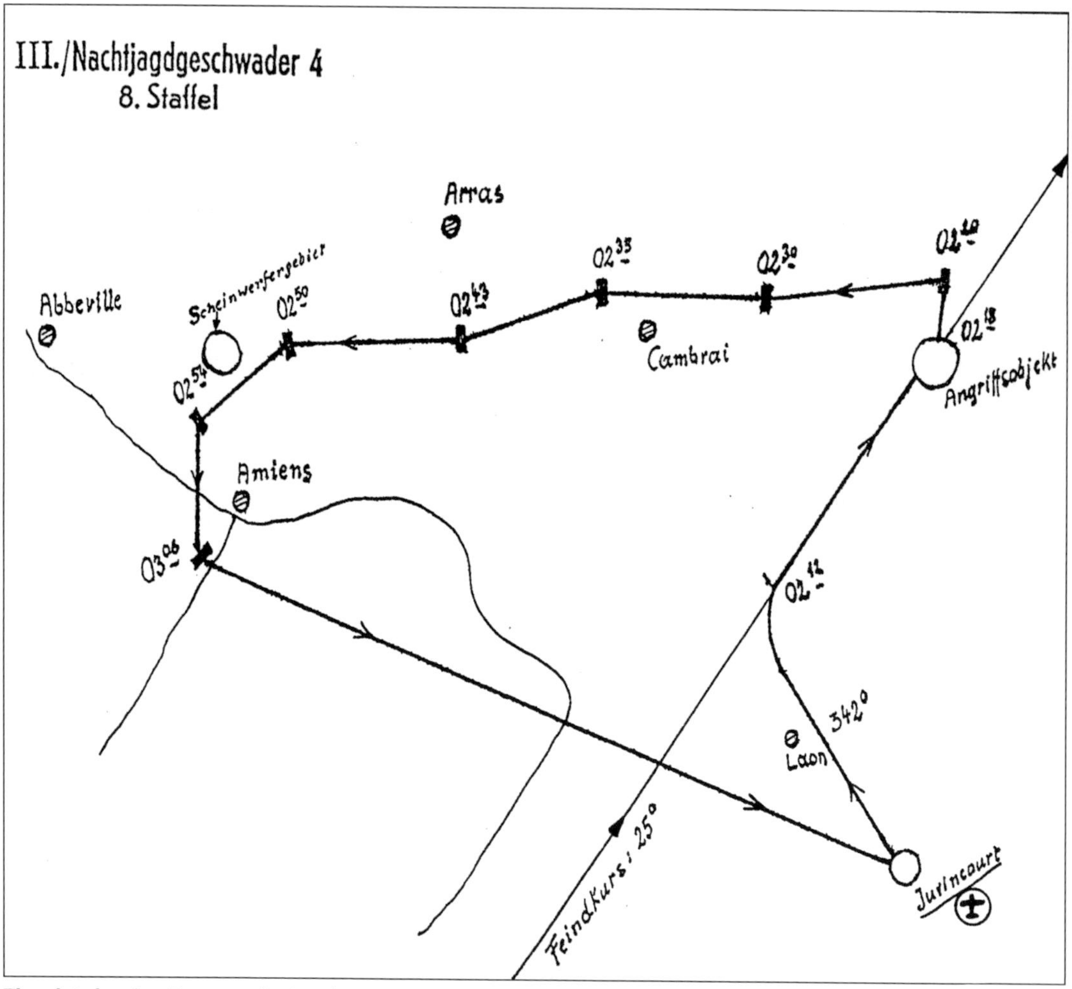

The plot showing Bergmann's victories on 11 April 1944.

Above left: Bergmann and his crew, 10 May 1944: Fw Wilhelm Schopp, Bergmann, Fw Günter Hauthall. All would be killed on 7 August 1944.

Above right: Now promoted to Hptm, Helmut Bergmann, April 1944.

Above left: Bf 110G-4 – similar to what Bergmann was flying when he was shot down.

Above right: Flt Lt John Surman of 604 Sqn, who is credited with shooting down Helmut Bergmann.

Other books you might like:

Historic Military Aircraft Series, Vol. 24

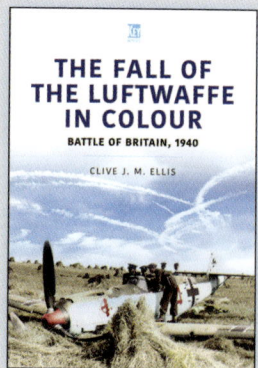

Historic Military Aircraft Series, Vol. 2

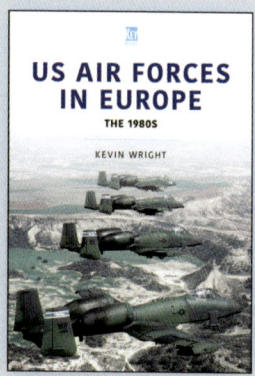

Air Forces Series, Vol. 4

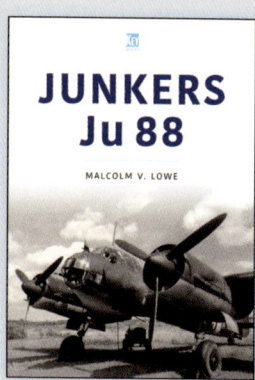

Historic Military Aircraft Series, Vol. 15

Historic Military Aircraft Series, Vol. 17

For our full range of titles please visit:
shop.keypublishing.com/books

VIP Book Club

Sign up today and receive
TWO FREE E-BOOKS

Be the first to find out about our forthcoming book releases and receive exclusive offers.

Register now at **keypublishing.com/vip-book-club**

Our VIP Book Club is a 100% spam-free zone, and we will never share your email with anyone else. You can read our full privacy policy at: privacy.keypublishing.com